THE WAY TO THE WAY

THE WAY TO THE WAY

By
Raphael Sidelman

Other books by Raphael Sidelman:

Think about it…

STRIVE

Perspicacious Press
Tijuana - Havana - Innsbruck - Nantucket - Kathmandu

The way to the way is an excellent guide to a personal philosophy that informs, teaches, and stimulates independent thinking about how to lead a more meaningful life. Mr. Sidelman pinpoints all of the pitfalls that keep us from the openness of fresh experience. He gives us basic precepts to follow, as well as cautions about remaining moderate, and in balance, as we follow them. Each chapter and sub-section is filled with an abundance of meaningful material. Through the skillful use of parables and illustrations, basic concepts are continually illuminated. The interesting ideas come upon us in quick succession, and we must stop to think and integrate before we can proceed. Mr. Sidelman's own suggestion that we read the book in the order it is written is very good advice.

While the historical origins of many concepts in this book are in oriental and Greek philosophy, it is very clear that these pages emanate from the author's very personal experiencing of the lessons that he shares with us. Each idea presented has been carefully considered and clearly developed. In addition, this book has a rather unique advantage of being, at the same time, intellectually stimulating and very understandably written.

I should recommend this book most highly to any thinking person who wishes to embark upon a journey of genuine self-discovery. Mr. Sidelman invites the reader to take this journey with him toward an informed observation of the world and one's place in it. There is much here to learn and relearn.

William J. Kirman, Ph.D., Professor Emeritus Dept. of Psychology

Long Island University, New York

Author of Modern psychoanalysis in the schools.

THE WAY TO THE WAY

I must thank the following for their help, support and input in regard to this book: Sybil Sidelman, Leslie Sidelman, Nicole Greener, Josh Sapodin, Ellen Haimoff, Norman Blinder, Hye Harris, Sondra Wolfe and her daughter Donna, Walter S. Wurzburger, David Leeds, Bill Kirman, Joseph Kelberman, Chaim B. Halberstam, Lloyd Schoenberg, Yaakov Lehrfield, Katie Olsen Zimmerman, George Varani, Scott Lopeck, Justine Zimmerman, Lao-Tzu, Steven Mitchell for his translation and interpretation of Lao-Tzu, everyone at Printing Dynamics in Rockville Center N.Y., the American Heritage Dictionary, Pat Ryan for the extensive use of his computer (I kept him from a lot of scrabble). And last, but most definitely not least, everyone who dismissed this book for one reason or another. Though unintended, your words enabled me to see aspects and possibilities that I was previously unaware of. Thank you.

Raphael Sidelman

Dear reader,

I feel as though it is important at this time to mention something that occurred during my attempts to have this book published, so as to illustrate a central premise of the book. One of the literary agents who found it unworthy of their representation gave this explanation for his disinterest: "I don't think it has the mystical qualities that are needed for the words to penetrate our souls". See, that's what's funny about humans, we are always looking for something more. Why should there be anything mystical about commentary on truth and its manifestations? Where mystical terms are used to portray truth, most people mistake the mystery for the truth. And once again the perception of truth is distorted and truth remains mysterious anyway. Can you say "religious ritual"?

Most people don't want the truth, they have been taught to prefer mystery. It enables them to comfortably continue their usage of the tools which reinforce the rationalizations that are the core of their perspective. We have an array of choices through which we might find this quite apparent. For instance, just look at what the majority of people do in their "spare time" (popular usage of this term exemplifies my point) and what they read; if and when they undertake such an endeavor.

My aim is to break this cycle, so as to enable people to become aware of the beauty and possibility which - although right in front of them in plain sight - are constantly overlooked and destroyed during their search for the mystical.

That having been said, I have one request before you begin your journey through my mind. Please travel slowly. You will find much more meaning within if you stop and ponder - taking every thing for what it is, rather than for what you might otherwise quickly perceive. If you must read certain passages over a few times, that is fine; I certainly have. Perhaps then, when you finally make sense of them, you will perceive of exactly what I am intending to communicate, as opposed to taking a glance and having "kind of" an idea about what I'm saying. When people *kind of* have an idea of what was intended or just is, interpretations become kind of misconstrued. This leads to incorrect thought and action. This leads to problems.

I did consider presenting my ideas in some type of cartoon illustrations, but I chose not to because that would have made the process of mental association too simple. When there is no effort required, regardless of the subject, human beings do not retain whatever it is that they might have learned.

R.S.

TABLE OF CONTENTS

I. Introduction. Pages I - III

II. Definitions. Pages 1d - 85d

1. Understanding.
2. Ignorance.
3. Instant gratification.
4. Balance.
5. Perception/perspective.
6. Selfishness
7. Values.
8. Money.
9. Accomplishment.
10. Parts.
11. Interrelationships.
12. Reinforcement.
13. Concepts.
14. Words.
15. Grey area.
16. Luck.
17. Truth.
18. Individuality.
19. Death.
20. Happiness.

III. Thought provoking composition. Pages 1 - 68

IV. Commentary. Pages 1/1a - 68/68a

INTRODUCTION

So many of the popular self-help books available tell us to relax and positively view whatever problems we perceive, whether or not the problems directly or indirectly affect us; and to learn from these situations and any people involved. But how are we supposed to positively view a situation, not to mention learn from it, if we do not already have instilled in us the how and why to positively view and learn from a situation? Simply telling someone that what they consider a problem is, in reality, no problem, doesn't work in the long term. Anyone who believes they have a problem has been taught to believe that whatever circumstances have presented themselves surely constitute a problem.

The foundation of thought involved in causing that person to believe a problem exists must first be re-established. Otherwise, we are basically telling people to apply paint as a means of fixing a crumbling structure. "Why," one might ask, "in reality is it not a problem? Everything I know tells me it is a problem." The problem is what we "know" and how we try to define and solve our problems. What we believe to be the formula for a cure is really what caused our problem in the first place; so the more of the "cure" that we apply to our problem, the worse the problem gets.

We try to solve our problems within the framework of our lives (existing perspectives, job, habits, etc.) but the problem is usually the framework itself. Our frames are assembled from pieces of other people's perspectives (parents, teachers, friends, the media), but they all have their own agenda which was created by the piecing together of their frames. Much of our framework is completed before we are capable of making a properly informed decision as to whether or not we believe such pieces will fit, or function, appropriately.

Once we are mature, or conscious enough to pick and choose from who and what we will incorporate ideas and perspectives, we must re-evaluate our entire framework from the ground up. "Are (did) these people who laid my foundation of thought, and give/gave me advice, living (live) what - after searching outside that realm - I consider a successful life? What are their values, and where do their perspectives lie? Why should I trust in, and limit myself to, their judgements?" (Now that I am capable of my own, and regardless of when their judgements were incorporated into my framework).

I

If everyone who was my elder knew what they were talking about, would we now live in such a deranged place? We cannot take words on faith, we must question. "What do I believe?" "Should I believe it?" "Why?" Why are your parents your parents? Because your father's sperm fertilized your mother's egg (with as much conscious help from either of them as you'd receive from a vending machine). Did this automatically prepare them to make correct decisions for you, or for themselves? It's easier to become a parent than it is to get a driver's license! Think of all the high speed collisions that occur every second on the highway of life because of improper parental guidance and peripheral interference. Ritalin and Prozac are not appropriate safety features within our mode of transport.

We are going to go back to the making of our collisions, first with truth, then with fellow drivers. Very simply, "The way to the Way" is set up like this: the first pages deal with definitions of what are the basis for many of our misconceptions. Next, we have thought provoking composition that deals with our attempts to negotiate the highway of life. Finally, there is commentary on the composition. The page numbers of the commentary correspond with the page numbers of the composition they are attempting to clarify. A number of pages in the commentary have words written vertically in their upper left hand corner, this denotes the existence of an acrostic within the structure of the corresponding work. Certain pages in the commentary itself also have acrostics incorporated within their structure, although there are no clues which signify their presence.

If you do not read this book in the order it is formatted, you will inhibit your ability to appreciate it.

This book is worth only what time and consideration you put into it. If you look through it quickly, it might provide you with a couple of neat quotes. If you invest the time and consideration equivalent to what you have in the past spent on the avoidance of your self (through tv, movies, games, social activities, etc...), this book will not simply expand some of your current perspectives; it will shatter them. But, I can guarantee you that this will not happen if you do not continually reread and ponder what is on these pages - to the extent that you have continually reinforced and compounded the misconceptions instilled in you since childhood. The words comprising this book are only signs to the actual Way. Living what they merely represent is the Way itself.

Bon voyage!

Please answer the questions on the following pages

Write down, in order, the five most important things in the world to you.

1.

2.

3.

4.

5.

If you had three wishes (you can't wish for more) what would they be?

1.

2.

3.

V

What are five things you know to be absolutely, unquestionably true?

1.

2.

3.

4.

5.

VI

Write down your definition of the following words: Good. Bad. Need. Know.

1.

2.

3.

4.

VII

Write down and explain who and what you are:

In order to go forward you must first go backward.

Yet when you then actually go forward you will appear backward

to those who are backward, yet think they are forward.

DEFINITIONS

An eager student one day approached the master, who throughout the land was renowned for his wisdom. The student asked: "Master, it is said by all that you are most wise. Please sir, there is a question which I and many others long to find an answer to, and some now believe an answer has been found; but I am not exactly sure. Could you tell me if their beliefs are correct?" The master offered to listen.

When the student finished his explanation of the question and its presumed answer, he looked up to the master with eyes not unlike those of a child eager to discover the gift he is certain to receive. After pondering for some time that which the student had spoken of, the master turned his gaze on to the young man; and then he spoke, four words were all he said. Four words. Four words with the strength of a hurricane, yet spoken gently as a summer breeze.

But the student looked back at him like a boy whose gift was nothing more than an empty box. "What do you mean you do not know? Your knowing is the talk of the land. It is said that your wisdom is beyond that of all other men!" replied the student. To which the master answered, "Perhaps. But if so, it was only through an awareness of my not knowing that the wisdom has been gained." Upon hearing this, the boy's look of discouragement quickly turned to one of wonder. He bowed to the master, showing his respect, then turned and left.

~~~UNDERSTANDING~~~

UNDERSTANDING

The master held an object in her hand and asked a student, "What is this?" The student replied, "Well master, that is obvious. You are holding a rock." "And what do you know of this rock?" asked the master. "What more need I know?" replied the student. "I am fully aware that it is a rock, and I fully know what a rock is." "Is that so?" asked the master. "You must then possess full understanding of the entire universe and all of its workings." "No master, not at all." replied the student, obviously quite taken aback. "I simply claimed to understand that rock." To which the master replied, "How can you make such a claim, when understanding of this object is only limited to the infinite relationships within which you might view it?"

UNDERSTANDING

We believe we understand a concept or situation and we form an opinion (perspective) which will affect any thought or action we take regarding anything we believe to be in any way related to that concept or situation. But what if our supposed understanding is mistaken? It is. Sadly, there is a misinformed conceptualization of understanding incorporated into the foundation of almost all of our thought and action.

The problem lies in how we form our supposed understanding. First of all, what constitutes understanding? Is it when we are able to compare whatever we are experiencing to something we have already experienced? Read about? Heard of? No. But unfortunately that is how we form our "understanding" of so many things. "It flies and has a beak, it must be a bird." But what is a bird? What do they do? What do they need? Are all birds the same? It's a tree, a river, a field, a woman. Wow, doesn't that make life easy! Just stay in your cave and blame everything on the bogeyman.

Figuratively looking at the word understand, what does it say? It says "stand under"; but these are incomplete directions to those in search of truth. To "stand under" is only one way of examining the whole. In order to properly examine the whole, you would have to stand under, over, to all outer sides of, inside of, while close, distant, and around all that is involved in the actuality of the whole, simultaneously for the entirety of its existence, under all possible circumstances; and this manner of examination is valid only for that which is tangible. Is it possible to do all of that?

Understanding is the awareness and acknowledgement of all that is related, and the appreciation of each component; not only in regard to a specific (your) situation, but in relation to all that is. So what do you understand? Considering what you understand, doesn't rushing ahead seem foolish?

~~~IGNORANCE~~~

IGNORANCE

"Such a foolish creature." said a student while watching a cat roll happily in the dirt. "How funny you should say that." said the master upon hearing the student's comment. "I often wonder if such creatures view our actions with the same irreverence." "But master, how could that be?" asked the bewildered student. "Are we humans not supreme in every manner of intellect? Look at all of the wonders we create." "Yes." replied the master, while looking at a billowing smoke stack and people hurriedly struggling to fulfill their desires because they mistakenly believe them to be needs. "I suppose we potentially are, but that is not the question. The question is how often we exercise our superior intellect. For if we have it but do not use it, are we not infinitely more foolish?"

IGNORANCE

Ignorance is not just a lack of understanding, although that is its foundation. Ignorance is action - including thought - based on false beliefs. No thing is until something creates division. Then, everything (which was originally no-thing) is born, creating unending need for discrimination. Meaning, once you name or separate anything, you must attempt to name and separate everything; and once you start, you can no longer, even if you try to put those same pieces back together, achieve the whole you were seeking when you first created division. The only way to remain "whole" is by not trying to define object through the subjective, which creates separation.

Once we divide and try to label anything (beginning with "I", "Me"), we must then divide and try to label the whole of reality into separate parts; because we - through our lack of understanding - bring into creation our own false concepts and create un-needed relationships dependent upon them, to which we become dependent. Everything can work with or without us and anything we do and perceive as an achievement. Our duality-based idea of achievement is actually nothing more than an added complication; because any "improvement" or "simplification" will only create a process of need for more "improvement" and "simplification" in order to perpetuate the alternate reality we have created, based upon our misconception. What improvements can you possibly make upon something you do not see the whole of, and therefore do not understand?

10d

~~~~INSTANT GRATIFICATION~~~~

11d

INSTANT GRATIFICATION

"Master," asked a student, "what is this instant gratification you speak of?" "It is like stepping over a dollar bill to reach a shiny quarter," replied the master. "But master," proclaimed the student, "surely no one would do such a foolish thing!" "Ah, but it happens all the time," said the master. "Could you give me an example?" asked the curious student. "Well," replied the master, "what of the multitudes of gluttonous people who bring about their own illness, or those who believe there is profit in polluting the water and air that their offspring must one day use?"

"I see now." said the student. "It appears that many people are constantly set back because of their desire to be instantly gratified." "Now that you have knowledge of instant gratification," asked the wise teacher, "can you give me an example showing that you also have an awareness of the interrelationships upon which it is dependent?" "Yes master," replied the student, "it is like one who is wandering, lost, simply because in their haste to arrive they did not bother learning how to recognize the ever-present information that would otherwise safely guide them." "Indeed." replied the master, smiling, "And if not instant gratification, what would you call it?" After a minute of focused attention the student answered, "I would call it 'unwitting embezzlement'." The master wiped a tear of joy from the corner of his eye and bowed deeply toward the student.

INSTANT GRATIFICATION

At least ninety eight out of each hundred times that we know there is something we must absolutely have or do, right now, we are mistaken. These are wants mistakenly believed to be needs. If and when this phenomenon is recognized, it is referred to as a desire for instant gratification. This desire for instant gratification is rarely recognized because it is a product of continual negative reinforcement from many different places. At the moment we are born, we seek instant gratification. This is not a bad thing; it is an inborn survival technique. We need to be held, we need food, and we need them now.

The problem starts a little, but not much, later; when we begin consciously manipulating others in order to satisfy our whims. We quickly learn by watching and listening to anyone older, the subtleties of body language, facial expressions, and voice modulation. As we grow and incorporate these tools into our physical repertoire, we are, though unaware, incorporating them psychologically as well. And through years of negative reinforcement, we come to believe that there is truth in what was rarely anything more than a tool used for false indication toward others. We actually become servants of what are now, through much repetition, unconscious cues whose original purpose was to have others serve us.

And let us not forget the fact that while all of the above is going on, we are also taking in and acting out many of the not so subtle, habitual aspects of those whose care we are under. Furthermore, we must include the role of our sense receptors. In time, physical pain and pleasure become seamlessly blended with psychologically perceived pain and pleasure. Who's to say, when we're not even conscious of it, where one ends and the other begins, or which caused the perception of the other?

Eventually we believe that we are bored and hungry and irritated and in need of things; when in fact we are not. Yet the fact that we are not and the reasons we think we are, remain mysteries. For they are rarely questioned; and if they are, it is rarer still that they are questioned outside of the sphere of their influences. So, by failing to evolve into creatures who are aware of what we do and why we do it, we devolve into creatures who act mostly upon what appears to be instinctual desire, but is not. And we continually reinforce the false concepts of random occurrence, luck, and parts, by quickly acting out (not only physically but also verbally) without an accurate awareness of the interrelationships which bring about those actions and their results.

Once we are mentally able, we must re-train ourselves to look at the extended affects and effects of what might transpire anytime we are compelled to believe in or act upon anything. We must do this so that when we are tempted by the possibility of quick gratification, we will recognize whether or not it is actually going to set us back. Remind your mind that if it is instant, it is probably "gratifiction"; not gratification. "Gratifiction" does not satisfy anything, it only helps negatively reinforce false beliefs and damaging habits. Look up the word fiction if you must. Furthermore, remember that on a figurative note, "gratifiction" takes the "A" out of gratification. When there is no "A" available to us, though readily available to others, what is our starting point? What becomes our point of reference?

The more you think about it, the more you'll realize that there is no such thing as "instantaneous".

~~~**BALANCE**~~~

BALANCE

A student asked the master, "Master, will you explain to me the concept of balance?" To which the teacher replied, "Certainly. In a static sense, which is the way most people view it, it is simply the coupling of the exact ratio of opposing forces within a given situation. Misapplication of this narrow definition accounts for much of the pain and sorrow in the world. In a realm such as our own, where there is any flux, balance manifests through a real-time accurate awareness of the existence of impermanence and the resulting correct interaction with all. The accurate real-time awareness of impermanence is achieved through an accurate awareness of the interrelationships which are inherently causing such coming and going."

"So," replied the student after a bit of contemplation, "because of their mistaken conceptualization of balance, most people's attempts at balance are akin to one who is content to jump from log to log against the current of a stream in order to avoid going over the edge of a waterfall. Although their attempts are inevitably temporary, they cling to the belief that those actions are correct; and when they or a loved one fail to achieve their objective, they place the blame elsewhere and continue along the same line of thought." "Yes." replied the master. "And what of those who are aware of the actuality of balance within flux?" "Well," answered the student, "they are not unlike one who accepts the fact that they will inevitably go over the edge of the waterfall, and rather than fight it, they figure out how to positively accord with it in order to not only survive the fall, but prosper from it." The master smiled and bowed her head toward the student.

BALANCE

Balance is possible only through awareness of the fact that everything is related. We learn to walk only when we realize the relation of right to left, up and down, forward and backward, and maintain a balance between those relative aspects in accordance with our goal. Until then we stumble in confusion. As children we learn the relation of our actions to the response they elicit; this is how we get what we want (unaware that our possibilities are limited to the choices made available by our parents or whomever is looking after us; a major factor in not only what mixture of components we attempt to balance, but also in how we act in our attempts throughout our lives).

If life is a struggle, then the struggle is for balance. Everything depends on balance - from molecular bonds, to our own proprioception. Even the physical universe is constantly changing to keep up with itself. If something - anything - changes, it invariably throws off the equilibrium of something else, unless they too change in order to compensate.

So, in other words, imbalance creates balance, and balance creates imbalance. This is the only way to maintain balance when there is any flux. There can never simply be static balance in the physical realm within which we exist. Attempts to step outside of this cycle (mentally or physically) are bricks in a wall that will inevitably collapse. In truth there is no way to separate balance from imbalance and vice versa. In reality they are complimentary aspects of the whole. Thus there is no way to accurately use either term. Living in positive accord with the law that governs such fluctuations is the only way to maintain what is for our purposes called balance; for as far as humans are concerned, our working definition of balance is really just a matter of positive and negative accord with that law as it manifests in our environment.

Positive and negative accord are recognizable only by recognizing the actuality of environmental homeostasis (referred to a moment ago as "the law that governs such fluctuations". i.e., the interplay of elemental energy). In this context, maintaining a healthy relationship with the law appears cut and dry: (1) Realize how our world functions. (2) Realize from that what is in our best interest. (3) Follow what is in our best interest. But, remember, humans are not physically built for pure objectivity, since we have nervous systems that make us aware of our own pain and pleasure (thus the need for ethics and morality). And this, of course, influences our beliefs regarding what a proper basis for ethics and morality actually is.

So, instead of trying to accord positively with our environment (i.e., maintaining balance), historically we have made up our own rules based upon human desire. This has caused our entire belief system to be independent from, and contradictory to, everything else which we are still an aspect of and whose law we are still subject to. In light of this, it appears that we must scrutinize our methods for the determination of what is actually pain or pleasure; since our perception of them is what will determine whether or not we are able to maintain "balance".

~~~~PERCEPTION/PERSPECTIVE~~~~

PERCEPTION/PERSPECTIVE

As two students were arguing a point, the master happened to enter the room with a book in his hand. "What is the cause of this disturbance?" asked the master. "Well master," replied one of the students while starting to point toward an object near a bookshelf, "he claims that is a storage bin, but I insist that it is used to bring water from the well. Since you are now here, could you please help resolve this issue?" "Certainly," replied the master, "let me just return my book to the shelf." As the two students watched, the master walked over to the bookshelf and picked up the object of dispute. He then turned it upside down, stepped up on to it, and returned the book to a shelf that was otherwise out of his reach. After stepping down, off of the object, he sat upon it and asked, "I'm terribly sorry to inconvenience you both; but could you please repeat your opinions again, for one as tired and old as myself?"

After seeing their teacher use the object in ways that were completely different from that of their dispute, both of the students simply looked at each other, confused. "What seems to be the problem?" asked the master. "It appears as though we are the problem master." said the previously silent student. "Obviously there is much we do not see. Perhaps we should put on our glasses." "No," replied the master, "they are already on. Take them off."

PERCEPTION

Perception is the acknowledgement and measurement by the mind, of stimuli from our sense receptors. Together, our five senses are the culmination of our sense receptors; but is what we perceive actually the entire picture? Or is it, perhaps, but a tiny distorted and distorting aspect? Upon receiving stimuli from the sense receptors, the mind will make an evaluation of the information based upon any known "pertinent facts". Beyond infancy these "pertinent facts" are often found, almost instantaneously, within our existing perspectives (i.e., that which had previously been learned), rather than by way of logical, open minded investigations into the true nature of what is being perceived and of that which is doing the perceiving; which is to say that our experiences are often influenced by what are known as preconceived notions.

The raw stimuli that's sent to the mind does not change, but the mind's acknowledgement and measurement of it does. For example: if as a child you are taught that insects are good to eat and you know you had them in your baby formula, and your parents and friends love them, and you are now fed buggy burgers (a great source of protein), your mind will acknowledge that, yes, a buggy burger is o.k. to eat; and it will then send all of the proper messages to all of the systems of the body responsible for digestion, to proceed. If, on the other hand, you have been taught that insects are yucky and should be avoided, if not eradicated, your mind will not let you get that burger anywhere near your mouth - whether it is au gratin, broiled, or fried. The smell will nauseate you. It will look disgusting. You will gag just by putting the "food" near your mouth. Yet the burger remains a nutritional gold mine.

Once our perception is influenced by our perspective, we can no longer perceive of things as *they* are. We acknowledge only what is pertinent in classifying them within a certain category or categories, in order to maintain our definition of reality

PERSPECTIVE

Perspective is both a product and a cause of all that we think, feel, and do. Our perspectives form while in the womb, and evolve until death. From the womb and into childhood, everything we taste, smell, hear, feel, see, and ingest, has a significant influence on our perspective. Then, at some point during childhood, the seemingly individual mind decides that it has an adequate understanding of the world around it and the ways it must interact with it, in order to survive and prosper. From that point on, everything we taste, smell, hear, feel, see and ingest is significantly influenced by our perspective. Our minds try to make sense of everything new by way of categorizing it within our existing perspectives. Only when we are confronted by something that we cannot fit within our existing perspective or add as an anomalous appendage, or outright avoid, do we expand our perspective.

As children, our perception of parents, family, teachers, some peers, and the media is that they are correct and to be trusted. Thus we are able to ingest much of what they say and do and make it part of our perspective without considering the veracity of it (not to mention that at this point in our lives we are unable to properly consider, let alone diagnose, the veracity of it). This misconception is the foundation of many misconceptions about one's self and the "world around us". As we grow, these misconceptions - which are now the foundation of much of our perspective - shape who and what we become.

~~~SELFISHNESS~~~

SELFISHNESS

While walking one afternoon, the master came upon two men squabbling. "Kind sirs," asked the master, "what seems to be the problem?" "He is selfish," proclaimed the first man, "he thinks of nothing but himself!" "Is that so?" asked the master, of the second man. "Well," said the second man, "why should I be obligated to help him simply because I have had good fortune and he has not?" To which the master inquired, "Has our unfortunate friend been derelict in his duties? Has he been acting foolishly despite wise council? Has he repeatedly forsaken his moral obligation to pay honest debts that he has accrued?" To which the second man replied, "Not that I am aware of. But I am aware of profitable opportunities that are now available to me, as a result of his misfortune." "I see." said the master. "This is not a case of selfishness at all. This man is not selfish." The second man smiled. The first man became angry and confused. "Master," asked the first man, "have you gone mad? He just admitted to seeing my misfortune merely as a profitable opportunity for himself."

"No sir, this is not madness, it is a case of mistaken definition. You see, this man obviously avoids the universal light of truth and is filled with darkness; which I will call non-realization. This is the cause of his apathy." Both men now looked confused, and the second man asked, "What do you mean?" While the first man asked, "Of what consequence is this to our dispute?" To which the master replied, "All seemingly separate things are actually connected. All physical forms are simply manifestations which emanate from the universal and unified Source of light in accordance with the law of duality and balance. Many, such as this man, are blinded by the allure of reflecting light as it shines off of seemingly independent forms. Thus, they are filled with the darkness of non-integrated awareness, which prevents realization of the actuality of self. The self is the essence of our integrated physical manifestation of the universal and unified Source of light. So I ask you, how can one who avoids that original un-differentiated light be selfish, not to mention successful in the long-term?" "So what are you saying I should do?" asked the first man. "Pity him," replied the master, "and ensure success in all of your future endeavors by way of maintaining an integrated awareness which supports actions that are in positive accord with the law of balance." Not long after, a look of wonder and relief came over the first man, while a look of fear came over the second.

24d

SELF (ISHNESS)

Selfish people are actually quite unselfish, and that's the root of the problem (actually our misrepresentation of concepts and mistaken word usage are the problem here, but...). People who are "selfish" are really looking for contentment everywhere but within their self. Yet in order for someone to actually be selfish, wouldn't they have to be completely occupied with their self? Paradoxically, anyone caught up in their self would be forced, by looking within, to expand their awareness of the world that appears to be "around" them. Looking within is the only way to see with clarity our actual integration with what otherwise appears to be outside of our physical being (reflected light presents a parallax). Therefore, people who do not see from within themselves cannot see beyond their limited and limiting imaginary boundaries.

By defining themselves according to their sense preceptor-based interaction and achievement (which is made possible by the lack of importance given to cultivation of self, and the importance placed upon cultivation of peripheral activity and material goods, by society), people see themselves as separate wholes and are oblivious to the interrelationships which enable all of reality. This causes people to act in what on the surface appear to be self-serving ways, but in reality is self-abandonment, and is thus self-destructive. And yet, since everything is, in truth, an interrelated whole, what can actually be individually self-destructive?

Do you know that when the bulb of a radish (the root) is not being adequately nourished the deficiency causes the leaves to grow, in order to gather more light? Humans do the same thing; but the leaves they grow or initially acquire (the latter most often being the case) are designed in reverse: not knowing how to adequately nourish the root, their leaves are capable only of dispersing reflected light in a failed attempt to shine.

*** Paradox; is that what happens when you castrate paradise?

(Through misconception, of course.)

~~~~**VALUES**~~~~

VALUES

"Master," asked a student, "how should one ascertain what is of value?" "Look toward non-domesticated animals." replied the master. "But sir, have we not labored for many centuries to distance ourselves and our habits far from those beasts?" asked the student. "Indeed," answered the master, "how else could we have honed our wants and desires to the dangerous point of jewels commonly representing a man, as opposed to the man representing a jewel?" "Master," replied the student, "I see your point about the man, as many relate to success and virtue. But why, of all things, should I look toward a wild beast in my search for proper value?"

"Why," asked the master, "do you suppose humans have such regard for those able to afford shiny trinkets and jewels?" "I suppose it is because those people have the means to afford them." answered the student. "But," replied the master, "is it not so that, often, attempts to obtain these arbitrary objects consume their awareness? And is it not so that the rituals performed in conjunction with the use of them also consume their awareness?" "Yes master, this is often the case." replied the student. "Well," asked the master, "might these actions and the beliefs which lead to and from them bring one closer to the path of truth?" "No master," replied the student, "they would not." "Then is it incorrect to say that these objects and rituals often have no practical use?" asked the master. "No master, it is not incorrect to say that often they do not have a practical use." answered the student.

"In this light," asked the master, "what difference do you see between humans and the beasts I advised you to look toward?" After a bit of contemplation the student smiled and said, "Non-domesticated animals place significant value only on what they need." "Thank you." replied the master, as he bowed toward the student.

28d

VALUES

Within a given time span there is only so much you can do. What is your priority?

The more exacting our ability to observe and represent time and concepts becomes, the more efficient we think we become at achieving that which we value. We are able to coordinate our efforts with those of another or others who share our values and can aid in their fruition. Or we can organize trade with those who simply have something we desire, or vice versa. Our values expand.

We can create commerce, government, laws, money, and religion. We can work overtime. We can make an appointment to have our car fixed. Pay our bills on time. Pay federal tax, state tax, city tax, county tax, sales tax, gas tax, land tax, and gift tax (if you're lucky enough, you will pay inheritance tax). We can watch tv, "surf the net", catch the train, catch a buzz, smoke a butt. We can equate character with assets. We can use and/or destroy everything else for profit. We can build prisons and fill them. We can create a bottom line and pay people ten cents an hour while we make millions of dollars. We can pollute because it is cost effective. We can ship our garbage elsewhere. We can pay our teachers less than one-tenth of what we pay our actors, and have generations of families on welfare because it's not worth it to educate them. We can buy on credit what someone else says is in style and cleanse our souls by donating - on the same card - to a worthy charity.

We can compete, compare, comply, and commiserate, but we can't contemplate - there's no time for it anymore. We can fall in love and get married and have kids and teach them values.

~~~~MONEY~~~~

MONEY

"Of what use is money, master?" asked a student. To which the master replied, "Money is potentially of much use, for it is not unlike a tool." "How so?" asked the student. "Well," answered the master, "money can enable you to accomplish what you otherwise might not, without its use." "Why then should I not endeavor to gather as much money as possible?" asked the student, "Would that not offer me the potential of any tool box?" "Indeed it might," replied the master, "but earning money takes an investment of time and energy which might be better spent. What need do you have for a diamond cutting wheel or calipers?" "I do not even know what they are." replied the student. To which the master answered, "So why invest the time and energy needed to buy them?"

MONEY

If time is money, then is money time? Is time money? No; money is a tool which can, in the case of material goods and certain physical activities, be substituted or exchanged for time. This exchange reveals our values of time and energy in relation to the acquisition of physical goods and/or the expenditure of physical activity.

For instance, if you go out to dinner you don't have to shop, cook, or clean. Not shopping, cooking or cleaning saves you time and energy, but it costs you money. The money was able to buy you time to do other things that you'd rather do. This is the exchange which reveals our values. Sure, eating out may have saved you two hours of shopping, cooking, cleaning, etc... But how much time and energy did you spend earning the money to pay for the meal? If it took you seven hours of work to pay for the meal but the meal only saved you two hours, in general, that is a poor exchange. (In general, because you may have gotten something else included, by paying for the meal. That something else could be anything from a piece of valuable information, to a wonderful sexual encounter). The ideal is to get out more than you feel you have put in. *Feel* you have put in.

Next to health, time is arguably the most valuable asset one can have; yet it can't be saved. Since it can't be saved, and it is a most valuable asset, we should spend it wisely. Doing only what you prefer seems to be the ideal way to spend (is it?), but it is very hard to do that on an extended basis anyway; because, at a minimum, we need food to survive. And since clothing and shelter are pretty much a must, we are usually forced to spend a portion of our time in search of the means required to provide them (i.e., money, by way of work). Herein lies one of the keys to getting the highest rate of exchange for your time and energy.

The ideal is to get the most and highest quality food, shelter, clothing, and long-term results while spending the least amount of time. Since it takes money to acquire food, shelter, and clothing, and it takes an expenditure of time and energy to get money, obviously we should aim to get the most money in the least amount of time. But, does the word most mean more than anyone else, or does it mean the most that you need? Does the highest quality mean the best available at any price, or does it mean the highest quality available to suit your needs? (Both your present and long-term needs) There are many "extras" available to us, at many different prices. What is their real value?

33d

Anyone can offer goods or services for a price, but only you can decide if they are a worthy investment. Is it worth working an extra fifty-nine hours to acquire that big tv and four head vcr? Or would you rather work only ten total hours and read a book? Should you lease that "hot" new car, and work an extra ten hours every week to pay for it, or should you simply get from point "a" to point "b" in the older, not so nice car? Or should you say "screw the insurance companies", and take a bus or a bicycle? How much better will my needs be served by the $120.00 name-brand pair of sneakers, as opposed to the well-made, no name pair for $29.00? How many pairs do I need?

Ask yourself, how much is too much? How much is enough? Am I being honest with myself, or am I just trying to keep up with everyone else? (Who are just trying to keep up with everyone else!) Is it worth it? Is there no more to life than simply acquiring things? Or is there a sense of self which takes precedence? Freedom.

If it is all about acquisition, then it will be difficult for you to ever achieve a high rate of exchange. You are a prisoner of those who set prices; not to mention those you are trying to impress. You want their product/acceptance/admiration, so you spend great amounts of time working to accumulate enough money to buy the desired products. Continuously. Even if you earn a lot of money per hour, you don't get ahead; because you must, and will, always purchase the newest, the best, and the most of it. The possibilities are endless (as are the payments).

A sense of self would preclude much of the frivolous spending which results in poor rates of exchange. A sense of self forces us to discover the real value of time. And it becomes apparent that acquisition is often a control-based illusion and a substitute for novel experience. We discover the value of our own ingenuity and realize how precious each moment of freedom is. When you are appreciating the natural beauty that is not merely surrounding you, but incorporating you, you learn the non-value (in terms of a need to acquire) of most everything else.

*** Remember: in business the "I" is silent.

34d

~~~~ACCOMPLISHMENT~~~~

ACCOMPLISHMENT

"Master," asked a student, "what is the most that one can accomplish?" "There is no limit to that which one can accomplish." replied the master. "How can there be no limit?" asked the student. "Are we not mere mortals?" "Yes," replied the master, "we are mere mortals; but accomplishment is only dependent upon values and imagination. The concept itself and all practices relating to it are man-made." "I will ponder your words master." said the student, curiously. "In the meantime, is there any further advice you might give me pertaining to accomplishment?" To which the master replied, "Seek carefully what you wish to accomplish."

ACCOMPLISHMENT

Our accomplishments are based on our values. What do you achieve compared to what you must sacrifice while in pursuit of your accomplishments? Are you sure?

Accomplishment	Gain	Sacrifice	Balance
Specify	Not just quantity, but how and why it's a gain.	Health, time, money, beliefs, energy, peace of mind, freedom, physical comfort, ecology, etc....	+/-

House (s)
Car (s)
Clothing
Furniture
Jewelry
Appliances
Assets (other)
Children (don't laugh)
Hobbies
Job
Love (mate/sex)
Friends
Pets
Meals
Creations (what you built, drew, wrote, or played, etc.)
Tools
Education (degrees)
Physical upkeep (sports, exercise, hair etc.)
Activities (movies, drinking, drugs, cigarette smoking, etc.)

38d

~~~~PARTS~~~~

PARTS

While traveling one afternoon, the master saw a man dumping trash into a stream. "Pardon me sir," said the master, "but why are you dumping trash into this stream?" "Of what business is that to you ma'am? You are not from these parts, or surely I would know you." replied the man. "What do you mean when you say, these parts?" asked the master. "What I mean," answered the man, "is that since you do not live near here, my actions are of no consequence to you." "If that is so," replied the master, "then surely your roof would not mind a few termites snacking on the ground floor of your home. Relatively speaking, are they not quite some distance apart?" The man thought for a moment and then said, "The roof, however distant, relies on the floor for stability and support. Termites eating the floor would eventually cause the roof to collapse."

"Yes," replied the master, "that is why you don't refer to your residence as your floor, roof, walls, toilet, sink, doors, furniture, and bed. You call your residence, which is comprised of those things, your house." "Yes," said the man, "collectively speaking, those individual things are my house. But what is your point, what does this have to do with the dumping of my trash?" "My point," replied the master, "is that collectively speaking, the items such as this stream, those trees, the ground and the sky which you consider individual, are no different than the plumbing, walls, floor, and roof of your home. They are inseparable facets of a greater home called Earth. My point is that there is no thing which is anything other than another aspect of a greater whole. The trash you dump is no different than the termites you despise, except for the fact that it causes greater harm. So now I ask, do you still believe that I am not of these parts and that your trash is none of my business?" After pondering for a few moments what the master had said, the man replied, "No. You are very wise and you have taught me to see that there are no parts. Parts is just a word; a tool to help us communicate distinctly about the whole. Never again will I mistake the tool for the object it was made to enhance. Thank you." "It has been my pleasure." said the master as she bowed and turned to go.

PARTS

What we refer to as our "five senses" - our sensors for the perception of stimuli from sources "outside" of our perceived selves - are there really five, or have we simply dissected five discernible features from what is in essence one indistinguishable whole?

Try eating when your nose is stuffed, and tell me how flavorful it is. How about judgement of dimension when you have an ear ailment, or feeling something without also incorporating sight; your perception of what you are directly feeling should still be the same, but what about your conclusion as to the actuality of what you are touching?

As with many other situations where the whole is broken into parts, when we refer to our "five senses" we enable the parts to expand beyond their actual scope. Of course this is only a matter of mistaken perspective; but unless we realize the mistake, it will appear as truth. The whole is originally broken into parts so that we can gain deeper insight into the subject at hand; but when it appears as though the parts individually have potential value, every attempt is made to exploit that perceived value. As the potential value of the "individual parts" are being exploited, the perception of the lines which inextricably connect the part to the whole fade and soon disappear. Now, even though the actuality of the situation is still that our mistaken perspective tells us there are parts when there is only an indistinguishable whole, we are no longer aware of it.

As a result of our efforts to maximize the potential of what we imagine to be individual parts, we see everything as a separate manifestation whose source, at its deepest, most defining level, must be tangible; which is why confusion abounds. Our misconceptions inevitably run into immutable law and instead of blending as like substance, they are repelled as is water from oil.

Any perceptible thing, whether or not it has form, has a Source. At its deepest, most defining level, its Source is the same Source as all that is perceptible and imperceptible. In order for interaction to properly occur, all conscious aspects must accept their role in relation to the Source; otherwise all interaction will be based on misconception. What is the manifestation of misconcepton? (i.e., what occurs when the i.e., which our actions are based upon is mistaken?) What is the inevitable result of imbalance?

41d

Figuratively speaking, what happens when you take the "w" out of whole? There becomes a hole. How? Why? Because the "w" stands for "double you"; meaning that, within the whole, you and everything else are, in actuality, reflections of each other. You are simply different physical manifestations of the same Source. When you fail to realize this, and there is no "double you", there is separation. You create a hole in what was complete. "ME" is an upside down "W" and "E", just as "WE" is an upside down "M" and "E".

~~~~INTERRELATIONSHIPS~~~~

INTERRELATIONSHIPS

One bitter cold day at the end of fall, a student visited the master. "Master," asked the student, "could you please help me gain awareness of interrelationships?" "Certainly." replied the master. "Go outside and pick an apple off of the tree." "O.K.," said the student, after he had gotten the apple, "what now master?" "Hand me the apple." said the master. When the student handed the master the apple, the master cut it into four equal sections. He threw the first one through a closed window, ate the second, tossed the third into a corner on the floor, and put the last section in a cup of water. After watching all of this, the student looked quite confused. "Come back in three hours," said the master.

When the student returned three hours later the master was sitting in the same spot, but with a heavy coat on. The room was freezing. "Come, take off your jacket and relax." said the master. "But master, it is freezing in here," said the student, "if I am to sit, I would prefer to leave my coat on." "Why do you think it is so cold in here?" asked the master. "I would think that it is because you threw that section of apple through the window before," replied the student. "I see." said the master. "It's funny how that happens, is it not? Come back again at this time tomorrow." When the student showed up the next day, the window was fixed but there was a pile of bodily waste on one of the two chairs in the room. After sitting on the clean chair, the master invited the student to sit on the dirty one, "Please, make yourself comfortable," said the master, "disregard the section of apple you picked yesterday." "But master," replied the student, "that is no longer an apple, it is excrement." "Yes." replied the master. "It's funny how that happens, is it not? Come back in one week."

The next week, when the student returned, the master asked the student, "Could you please do me a favor?" "Anything, of course," replied the student, "what is it?" "I had forgotten something in that corner over there," said the master, pointing, "would you be kind enough to bring it to me?" "Of course." replied the student. Upon walking to the corner, the student saw the section of apple the master had thrown there a week earlier; it was covered with mold and was attracting ants. "Master," said the student, in shock, "it is that section of apple you threw here last week.

44d

It is covered with mold and is attracting ants. I don't want to pick this up with my bare hands." "Indeed." said the master. "Is it not funny how that happens? Come back in two weeks."

Two weeks later, when the student showed up, the master was sitting at his table studying a tiny plant in a pot. "Hello master," said the student, "should I come back at another time? It is obvious that you are busy." "No." replied the master. "Please, come sit down." When the student sat down, he too began looking at the tiny plant. "What are you growing master?" asked the student. "This is the section of apple I put in my water glass three weeks ago." replied the master. "Please, take it home and replant it in the spring, so that you may have many examples of interrelationships to ingest for years to come." Upon hearing and seeing this, the student was in a state of wonder. "Master," said the student, "you have taught me much regarding interrelationships in the last few weeks. I have come to realize that not only does any action elicit a response, but I see also that nothing ends. There are no dead end streets; for every action is the result of an intersection, and each reaction in turn creates many intersections. I see also that the ability to perceive beauty is limited only by our inability to gain awareness of the complexity of the relationships inherent in even the seemingly simple. I now realize that nothing just happens. Thank you master for this multitude of gifts, it is as though the universe has expanded." To which the master replied, "Funny how that happens, is it not?"

INTERRELATIONSHIPS

Try to visualize an uncountable number of doors which are constantly, seemingly without reason, opening and closing. Visualize that each door, whether open or closed, provides a pathway of possibility in your life. Realize that the doors continue to open and close without any action or effort on your behalf. Even in unconsciousness, the doors of possibility are moving. Realize that each entity everywhere has an uncountable number of doors representing their possibilities, which are opening and closing constantly, with or without consciousness, seemingly without reason; but, you are one of the reasons. Now try to visualize everyone and everything doing everything they ever do. Realize that they are hinges on your "doors" and that their actions, in addition to your own, are what cause your pathways of possibility to open and close (and vice versa).

In your wildest imaginings you could not visualize what events actually brought you and the person behind you on line at a store, to that place at that exact time. Everything is interrelated. The fruition of everything you ever do is dependent on possibilities made available and secured through the negotiation of interrelationships. Being conscious of and acting in positive accordance with your limitations is to utilize a light which illuminates darkness. With light you can see and avoid what might have otherwise set you back, or caused injury. All failure is the product of incomplete awareness.

~~~**REINFORCEMENT**~~~

REINFORCEMENT

"Master," asked a student, "why do some un-natural things feel natural, while some natural things do not?" The master answered, "This is because of reinforcement." "What exactly do you mean?" asked the curious student. "What I mean," replied the master, "is that through continued practice, any thought or action will appear natural. The same applies to non-thought or inaction, because the more one does of anything, the easier it gets; just as the less one does of anything, the harder it becomes to do." "Master," asked the student, "among the infinite possibilities, how might one properly discern what to reinforce?" To which the master answered, "By consciously being in constant harmony with the unchanging law of balance."

REINFORCEMENT

All action creates more action. As any action creates more action, each action will in turn cause reinforcement. There are two forms of reinforcement: positive and negative. The form of reinforcement produced by any particular action will in turn enable more of the same type of reinforcement to occur. Positive reinforcement compliments homeostasis, negative reinforcement defies homeostasis. The more you do of anything, the easier it gets. The less you do of anything, the harder it becomes to do. Positive reinforcement compliments homeostasis, negative reinforcement defies homeostasis. In most cases, what seems "natural" is really just what has become familiar and easy. Positive reinforcement compliments homeostasis, negative reinforcement defies homeostasis. Just as smoking a cigarette (negative) feels natural to one who regularly smokes, proper physical exercise (positive) seems natural to one who regularly exercises. With practice, either person could come to feel as though either habit is natural; yet neither is. They are both what has, through continued practice, become familiar and easy.

Misinterpretation of concepts through the use of words is how the majority of negative reinforcement occurs. If you tell a lie often enough, you eventually believe it. The line between truth and fiction becomes faded and before you know it, it's gone and you are unable to differentiate between the two. When we misrepresent a concept through improper word usage, such as saying "need" instead of "want", we are reinforcing the negative (false) belief that the want is actually a need. The more you do of anything, the easier it gets. The less you do of anything, the harder it becomes to do. The word "natural" is another fine example. Is what's natural necessarily healthy for us? Everyone seems to think so. How did this happen? Lead is natural, so is uranium; are they healthy for us? The word natural is constantly, erroneously used to cite the concept of health. Everything natural is not healthy for us; but since the word "natural" is so often used to represent what people want us to believe is healthy (so we'll buy), and since we accept and incorporate their purposely mistaken usage into our own, we no longer see any difference between the two. When we do this, the misrepresentation becomes our basis for truth. Judgement is based upon perceived truth. Think about how many facets of your life have been and continue to be shaped in this manner: good, bad, beauty, ugly, smart, stupid, new, old, superior, inferior, strong, weak, hard, easy, need, want, improvement, asset, wealth, success. Then think, "What am I going to do about it?" Positive reinforcement compliments homeostasis, negative reinforcement defies homeostasis. The more you do of anything, the easier it gets. The less you do of anything, the harder it becomes to do.

~~~~CONCEPTS~~~~

CONCEPTS

A young widowed mother came to the master. "Please sir, I must ask your advice. My son is fifteen and he refuses to go to school or work, I love him but I cannot support his habits." The master thought for a moment and then said: "For the next week, every day that your son continues his refusal set aside one dollar for him." The young mother was shocked. "Master, surely you jest! I barely have enough money to pay my rent." "No," said the master, "do as I say for one week; then send your boy to see me, with all of the money in his hand."

One week later the boy showed up, money in hand, embarrassed to see the master. "Hello!" said the master, smiling. "I see that you have had quite a profitable week. How is it that you earned your handful of money?" The boy, unable to look the master in his eye, said sheepishly, "I have done nothing to earn this money; my mother gave it to me." "Well done." said the master. "Even kings must provide safety to their subjects in order to collect taxes. If only you could expand on this method somehow, you might live better than a king." "Master," said the boy, "I know you mock me with your words, but it does not seem fair that I should have to do things in life which I so despise." "Well," said the master, "do you think that you are alone in your quandary?" "No." answered the boy, "I do not." "No. You are not." replied the master. "There are plenty of parasitic people and thieves who feel exactly like you do. But there are also people like your mother who carry on productively, simply because they are aware of the negative consequence inherent in their inaction."

The boy looked puzzled. "Do you think anyone really enjoys wiping themselves after defecating?" asked the master. "No." said the boy. "I would think not." "So," replied the master, "why then don't we all complain that it is unfair and simply go about our business without having done it?" "Sir," said the boy, "I imagine that would cause a situation worse than the one we were trying to avoid." "So," asked the master, "what do you suppose is the difference between that and the effect of your refusal to do what you claim is not fair?" The boy pondered for a few moments and then spoke, while finally looking the master in the eye. "Thank you master for opening my eyes; I must go now, for there is still daylight under which I might work, so as to begin repaying my mother for the sacrifices she has made because of me." "It has been my pleasure." said the master. "May all of your efforts be blessed with the beneficial responses that follow properly informed action."

CONCEPTS

Our lack of familiarity with the actual basis of individual concepts is a major contributing factor to our confusion. Even if we look a word up in a dictionary, we rarely get more than a comparison to something else which is used as an example to illustrate what the concept is. That method of definition does not expose for scrutiny, the actual foundation of thought involved in the basis for belief of such concepts. Yet we use the word. Only when we visualize the essential aspects of a concept can we begin to see what interrelationships are actually involved. Only by studying the interrelationships that are affecting, and that are affected by, a certain concept can we recognize its validity.

The lack of attention paid to the importance of our familiarity of concepts has been made quite convenient for us. Under the guise of ensuring efficiency and convenience, in order to make the most of our limited time, we are taught to try to abbreviate everything possible. And even the methods for determination of the applicability for abbreviation have been abbreviated. We don't have to read any fine print (including that of our own lives); we pay others to do that for us. We pay others to condense all of the fine print into one neat headline. And when a problem develops we can pass the buck, and pay to have others *attempt* to fix it.

Where do all of these short cuts leave us? Has this really empowered us as advertised? Or have we actually weakened our own essential abilities, by giving other people and things the power to so easily influence us without inquiry?

53d

54d

~~~~WORDS~~~~

WORDS

"Master," asked a student, "what are words?" "Words," replied the master, "are symbols through which we visually and verbally express concepts." "And what is their value?" asked the student. "That is dependent upon the concept they represent, and their success in being able to convey the concept." said the master. "How so?" asked the student. "Well," answered the master, "if a concept is incorrect, would the sounds and symbols used to express it not be like counterfeit money? And if the concept was correct, but those trying to convey it were unsuccessful, of what value were the words?" "I see." said the student. "Words are like most cans. Their value is in proportion to what they contain and how accessible those contents are."

WORDS

Since words represent concepts, word usage enables us to unconsciously take concepts for granted and continually reinforce our misconceptions. This contributes to the continual compounding of our perspectives being off center.

For example, look at the way "beauty" is portrayed by all forms of media, and continually pushed into our minds. Our definition of it gradually becomes what we are being shown and thus told, when we repeatedly see and hear the names and images of any product this "beauty" represents and promises us: money, status, peace of mind, muscles, sexy, thin, new and improved. We accept the subtle messages that even tv's and cars can enable us to be beautiful, simply by our being associated with them. This is accomplished by the manufacturer having their products shown to us in concert with established forms of beauty when advertised (i.e., a certain quote, music, pictures, people, or combinations of these together). Through our being bombarded with the implication that there is such a thing as beauty by association (which is made much easier to find than our innate beauty - any brand name will do), one's role as a consumer is expanded way beyond that of hard goods. Our search for meaning and self-worth is no longer taken within; it is done in stores and in "holy places" (notice the lack of a double you), through catalogs and on the web.

Once we incorporate this concept of commercial beauty into our vocabulary, it traps us; because it eliminates, through negative reinforcement, the concept of innate beauty (see "Gratifiction"). Now the only way to become, and maintain, beauty is by association with what we are told are beautiful things. Our own actions and beliefs can no longer be beautiful or valuable. Only those things which claim to represent established beauty can be beautiful or valuable. When we buy into the idea of commercial beauty, we become prisoners of those who have something to sell. And who doesn't have something to sell? Most people can't buy anything until they are convinced that they've sold it to you.

We aren't even aware of this being done because the process is subtle, continuous, and interactive. Yes, it is possible to be subtly bombarded.

As a matter of fact, you have been and will be subjected to many forms of this throughout your entire life. Since the dawn of verbal communication, down through each generation, it has included everything from sneakers to religion. Realize that we are drawn into this process at a very young age. It is taught to us by the people we learn language from. Then ponder this: just as a step one-degree off course will, after one thousand miles, bring you many miles off course, one word used incorrectly one thousand times will do the same. You are not simply using the word, you are misrepresenting a concept. After a while, your definition of the concept will be whatever you made it. And since your definition of your self is directly related to that, where will this leave you?

~~~GREY AREA~~~

GREY AREA

"Master," asked a student, "what is grey area?" "Grey area is the fifth ace in a deck of cards." answered the master. "But master," said the student, "there is no fifth ace in a deck of cards." To which the master replied, "Precisely."

GREY AREA

Grey area is not the acknowledgement of not knowing right from wrong/correct from incorrect. It is a mental construct based upon the belief that even with a properly informed perspective, right and wrong/ correct and incorrect are either not discernible or not unlike one another enough to make a meaningful difference. Grey area is possible only when our conceptualization of interrelationships and balance is limited. Only a limited concept of one would enable us to believe that the other is limited; meaning that it is not always applicable. How else could our perspectives go outside the parameters of such elemental guidance?

Grey area is a double edged sword and a Pandora's Box. Just as we use it to our advantage, so do others; and who are we to condemn those who do as we do? There becomes a rift in consciousness through which anyone can push their agenda. Excuses and distorted perspectives become acceptable representations of truth. Then truth is based upon whatever distorted perspectives were allowed to portray it. And all parameters upon which perspective is based shift accordingly, in what becomes a cycle of distortion. Yet, through all this, the truth remains the same.

What would you call a person who tried to live what is mere fantasy? Delusional. Grey area is delusion.

~~~~LUCK~~~~

LUCK

"Master," asked a student, "how might one become either lucky or unlucky?" To which the master replied, "By using either word." After pondering for some time what the master had said, the student asked, "I cannot fathom your explanation master, could you please present it in a different way?" To which the master replied, "Luck is our way of admitting our limitations without having to recognize them."

After pondering the master's last statement, the student spoke. "Thank you master, I am now aware of the nature of luck." To which the master replied, "Well, how might you now tell another to become either lucky or unlucky?" "I would tell them to disregard all concepts relating to interrelationships." replied the student. "Thank you." replied the master, as he smiled and bowed toward the student.

LUCK

Luck and fate are not forces, they are simply words used to cite the unfolding of events that we don't understand. Everything that happens is a result of what has happened, or is happening; we are just unable to fathom the relationships involved in the fruition of such happenings.

~~~**TRUTH**~~~

TRUTH

"Master," asked a student, "why do people find the truth to be so elusive?" To which the master replied, "Because they are trained to not see it. If and when they fleetingly perceive it, they consider it a mental lapse." "I am sure I do not fully comprehend the details involved in your explanation master, could you please be more specific?" asked the student. "It would be my pleasure," answered the master, "please, have a seat." Once the student sat, the master said "First, realize that I am not going to expound upon the many symptoms associated with lack of awareness of Truth, which compounded will further distance one from its realization. Rather, I shall go directly to the root, the symptoms are other lessons." The student nodded his head and the master began.

"By believing that there is a supreme entity separate from our reality, who simply looks on and occasionally directly affects us, or that there is such a thing as random occurrence, we, in our minds, limit the actuality of the Source; and we enable the existence of rationalization and the illusion of control. We are able to make attempts at finding something better than the actuality of the natural world. We make things of 'beauty' rather than expanding our awareness of the beauty which already exists anywhere we look. We live our lives as if we were trying to find a present hidden beneath wrapping paper in a box, but our reality is that of the wrapping paper and box which we tear apart and discard. We never see the Truth because we are too busy searching for something else which does not exist.

"For our purposes in this realm - the physical realm - we must gain awareness of the fact that everything is but an illusion if we take it at face value. We must learn to transcend the titles attached to people and objects, because these titles limit our awareness of the actual interrelationships involved in our combined existence. When titles no longer obscure the nature of things, which is to say that one realizes everything is just a variation of everything else - all of which is connected - it becomes apparent that there are many layers of misunderstanding embedded in the public and private consciousness. Hence, the busy search.

"If people realized that the God they seek is the essence of the physical reality known as the physical universe, including all of the seemingly specific forms, they would treat everything with the reverence they reserve only for the God they have never consciously encountered. Thinking of God as a separate entity is a result of fragmented perspective, which is a result of differentiated consciousness. When we go beyond differentiated consciousness we realize that God doesn't judge us. God is undifferentiated consciousness or, put another way, Universal immutable law. We, all things, physically react to Universal immutable law in accordance with our physical nature, in relation to the nature and intensity of our interaction with each other. It does not react to us. It just is. God, the Source, Universal immutable law, and Truth are simply different names for what is the same.

"When we react in positive accordance to the whole, rather than reacting toward what is only partial (perspective), we don't simply emulsify with Universal immutable law (the Source, God, Truth), we blend as selfsame energy and effort is no longer required. When we react to the partial, life is a struggle. In order to control something, you must master it. In order to master something, you must become that thing. Realize that all things physical are simply mutated manifestations of the Source and that it is only through positive accord with the Source that you can positively relate to its manifestations. Trying to positively relate to the Source only through its manifestations is not possible, because you will always be trying to make the partial complete by way of partiality; using the same tools which created the partiality in the first place. But you cannot fix a problem by inducing more of what caused the problem. $0 + 0 = 0$. The actions, movements or rhythms that are eternal are in positive accord with Universal immutable law. The Source. God. Truth. Everything else is in negative accord - by way of partiality - which is why they don't last in that form.

"Thinking that we are able to judge because we understand is like watching one split second of an event and thinking that we saw its entirety. Thinking that the event is, in itself, an entirety is the same thing. In the actual scheme of things we don't see any beginning or end. Every thing is the unfolding of one original "particular" action which will continue until the finite has run its course. The creation of all things is simply that one action running its course. All things that have happened since that action are but a continuation of that action, which is commonly known by the name 'reaction'. Those reactions are always in accordance with the actuality of Universal Immutable Law. The Source. God. Truth."

After pondering what the master had said, the student replied, "Thank you master, I am now aware of why the truth eludes so many people. The foundation of their basis for judgement is distorted, and this results in the further compounding and distortion of their perspective. There is nothing hidden. It is we who hide. But master, I must ask, why did you say earlier, 'For our purposes within this realm – the physical realm...?'" "I am pleased that you thought to ask me that," replied the master. "I said 'for our purposes within this realm, the physical realm...', because although Universal immutable law is the essence of all of this, what we can palpate is not all of *It*.

"Would you claim that a wave is the entire ocean? No. The wave is as much the ocean as any other aspect, but it is incorrect thinking to believe that every nuance there is to learn about the ocean may be culled from a wave. Although we are capable of spiritually transcending our physical limitations, our existence within physical form and our having to yield to the immutable laws which apply to all physical form is still a specific, limited aspect of the entire limitless actuality within which we exist." And then he asked the student, "So what is right and wrong within this realm?" The student looked perplexed and simply shook his head as if to signify that he did not know. The master then spoke. "In this realm, anything which is in positive accord with natural environmental homeostasis is right. Anything in negative accord with it is wrong.

"Right and wrong are not a matter of some biblical doctrine, which tells us that through the course of certain miracles it is our right to be here. Right and wrong are simply dependent upon the eternal rhythms which are the laws of the universe. How am I aware of this? Because anything that does not maintain balance will not endure." "So," replied the student after a bit of contemplation, "nothing is intrinsically good or bad; and anything can potentially be used for good or bad. Even what is good in one situation can be bad in another, and vice versa. Everything just is; it is we who make good and bad." "Precisely." replied the master. "All walls are doorways, and all doorways are walls. All pathways are obstacles, and all obstacles are pathways. All darkness is light, and all light is darkness. Do not mistake the words 'good' and 'bad' for that which is right or wrong".

TRUTH

We look at particular happenings and base our idea of truth upon them. By this method, any particular action creates its own truth. This causes the existence of many conflicting truths. Conflicting truth is what allows everyone to substantiate the validity of their beliefs, which in turn substantiates the validity of their actions. Truth becomes a matter of opinion.

All things true are not truth. Yet all things are, in some sense, true. For everything, once conceptualized, is (in some form of existence). But this fact of existence does not automatically qualify as truth. Truth is not dependent upon circumstance.

With the introduction of the concept "true", everything (including truth) became true. Yet, in all of actuality, only truth would exist without differentiated consciousness. Even "reality" is not truth. Reality is simply the sum of all that is true, which is why there are unlimited manifestations and, in accordance with specific situations, numerous definitions correctly referred to as reality; but, although truth is their essence, as it is the universal essence, they cannot be functionally referred to as truth. Truth is the immutable law of the universe. Truth is undifferentiated consciousness. Differentiated consciousness (i.e., the realm of duality; i.e., reality) is everything else.

.

~~~INDIVIDUALITY~~~

INDIVIDUALITY

The master said, "There is nothing which has not been affected. There is nothing which can be affected without other subsequent affect." To which a student replied, "But master, what of a singular isolated instance?" "There is no such thing." answered the master. "For we exist within a unified whole".

INDIVIDUALITY

When we first look within, we see darkness. This is because we have been taught and made to seek artificial light outside ourselves, as a substitute for the original light which exists within us all. But if we take the time to search the darkness, a sense of self develops and we begin to see the first hints of light. The light appears weak and dim, but that is an illusion; we are very far from the Source. As we approach the Source - through the study of our self - the size and intensity of the light grows. But this is not because we have increased the light. It is simply because we have moved closer to it. The light cannot be affected by us. It is we who are affected by the light.

The light is truth. Though we search individually for the light, the light we find is the exact same light in every one of us. And although we find it only by looking within, it is we who are within it. When you get close enough to the light to see what it actually is, you see what you actually are. And you realize that we - everything - are all intrinsically the same; just physically altered manifestations emanating from the same Source, all connected*.

We are not just of the same light, we are the same light. When you go deep enough within your self to accurately perceive the light, you will see that "everyone" and "everything" is there, *with* you.

*Think about the word "connected" for a moment, while being aware of this fact: the word that we use to indicate the attachment of otherwise separate things is one of the tools that prevents us from becoming aware of the fact that there are, in actuality, no separate things. Without the belief that there exist things that are not connected, the word "connected" would not exist.

Think about it: in-divi-duality - not divisible duality.

Even the word we use to represent being separate is telling us that attempts at separation are a mistake. We are a non-divisible duality; a "double you"; reflections of each other. "ME" is an upside down "WE" and vice versa.

~~~**DEATH**~~~

DEATH

"Master," asked a student, "what is death?" To which the master replied, "Loose change is death." After pondering the master's statement for quite some time, the student asked the master "Master, I am sorry to say that I see no correlation between death and loose change, could you please explain further?" To which the master replied, "Loose change is money in a form different from that of a dollar bill. To the partial mind, the dollar bill represents a complete whole. Loose change is the result of the breaking down of that complete whole." "But master," replied the student, "no one fears the result of the breaking down of a dollar. They know there will be change, whether it be in coin or represented by what they have purchased."

"Yes," replied the master, "people are able to see and hold and save and control exactly what will happen to the resulting change of their dollar. It is their inability to realize that there is no way, and certainly no need, to see, hold, save, and control exactly what will happen through the resulting changes that are an inevitable aspect of their existence which causes much of their fear. The rest comes from not accepting that the actuality of what we call death is simply the inevitable breaking down of our current physical form into other changed form. Even if one chose to not spend their dollar, it would eventually turn to dust." "Master," said the student after some time, "I am now aware that death is nothing more than another name for one of the many imaginary lines which are drawn when one thinks in partial terms. When one sees beyond partiality, they are aware of the inevitable constant change which balances the whole. They have no fear of the change because they acknowledge their relation to the whole; which is to say that they are aware of the fact that nothing ends. But I still have one question regarding this subject master. What is the explanation for a violent or unnatural death?" To which the master replied, "That change is the immediate result of a negative accord with immutable law. Certain actions which are in negative accord with immutable law result in grave immediate consequence." "Thank you master." said the student, as he bowed and turned to go.

DEATH

Look up the word "death" or "dead" in a dictionary and you will probably fear it: *Extinction; Termination; lacking some important or previously evident quality.* But these explanations to the question of death are false claims. Nothing actually begins and nothing actually ends. Every seemingly separate thing is a continuation. The concept of connectivity is a contrivance which exists only in the realm of duality. It is only the form which changes.

In that light, aren't "life" and "death" the precursor of one another? In that light, wouldn't any new life require death? Wouldn't that prove the prevailing definition of death inaccurate, since all new life is incorporating the supposed "dead" into itself in what is but a changed form? And wouldn't that be akin to the argument of which came first, the chicken or the egg? Life needs death just as death needs life. This is no different than any other cycle, except in our minds which create tragedy after having been taught that we are somehow superior and thus exempt from the laws by which all else must abide. Why would we be any different than everything else, all of which is recycled?

~~~~**HAPPINESS**~~~~

HAPPINESS

Upon seeing a man weeping near a tree, the master walked over to him and said, "I am sorry to see you in such a way sir. Is there anything I might do to help rectify your situation?" To which the weeping man replied, "Thank you kind sir, but no, I don't think there is any way to help me. I have simply lost my eye for all beauty in the world, and am constantly without joy." The master replied, "I see." And then, while pointing to an old crooked willow tree, asked, "Sir, do you notice that tree?" "Yes, of course I do. Why?" answered the man. "Well," said the master, "that tree has been climbed upon, cut, bent by the wind, burned by the sun, frozen by ice, starved without rain, urinated upon, and invaded by uncountable creatures, yet it not only lives on, it attempts to flourish!"

"Yes, but it is only a tree." said the man, "It knows of no better." "Really?" asked the master. "Has it not lived many days in fine warmth, with plentiful water, and no infestation?" "O.k.," answered the man, "it probably has, but what is your point?" "My point," said the master, "is that although it may have experienced ideal conditions, the tree is not hampered by expectations of them. It simply accepts what is out of its control. But you believe you know better. Since you feel as though you know better, when events do not occur in accordance with your expectations, you feel sorry for yourself.

"You see, when people think that they are able to comprehend cause and effect, they begin to form perspective. When people begin to form perspective, they begin to have expectations. They are fooled by their perspective, which presents the illusion of separation; this causes them to see objects, events, creatures and people as separate wholes upon which circumstances can be randomly presented. All of this happens at a very young age and is continually compounded. Only when we recognize that we cannot comprehend cause and effect are we able to see beyond the illusion of separation and random occurrence. And only then are we able to perceive of how toxic and futile our expectations are; because it is then that we gain awareness of the fact that there are myriad interrelationships which constitute the whole of reality. We realize that we are an infinite aspect of the universal flux, and we no longer involve ourselves in struggles to attain quantifiable evidence of our success. As a matter of fact, we recognize that all measurement is but a relative guide.

82d

Measurement requires comparison. Comparison that is not rooted in an awareness of its own limited frame of reference creates a need for further separation. And yet, the separation creates paradox because of its lack of complete awareness. Paradox creates confusion and fear. And it is confusion and fear which create the "need" for measurement.

"Through all of the ensuing unfair action which takes place in our minds because of false beliefs, and creates misery through countless let downs and setbacks, how could we not feel sorry for ourselves?

"Not feeling sorry for itself, having no expectations, the tree is able to rejoice in even the tiniest blessing." After pondering the master's words for some time, the man smiled and said, "Thank you kind sir, our conversation has been a blessing. I now see that happiness is not a matter of events, but a matter of how I view those events. I believe this realization will enable me to appreciate many of the gifts I have previously overlooked." "Thank you." said the master, as he bowed and then turned to continue his journey.

HAPPINESS

Happiness is available to everyone. We just have to be taught the way to find it. If people can be taught to believe that there is virtue and a sense of pride to be found in "paying their fair share" of income tax at the end of their work week (by way of it being confiscated before they are issued a paycheck), they can be taught to accept and accord positively with truth. If all of the time and energy that is spent on continuing our ability to rationalize our mistaken ways were spent on being able to live harmoniously with our "surroundings" and our self, we would have no problems.

We would see that we create all of our own problems. We would see that all of our problems are simply a matter of perspective. We would realize that since all of our problems are simply a matter of perspective, there need be no problem.

We imagine that our own perspective regarding an event is truth. We are not aware of the fact that our perspective is based upon misconception. When we become aware of our misconception, we realize that the only thing getting in the way of our happiness is the way we have learned to pursue happiness.

Those truly determined to change are both the blacksmith *and* the iron. Flames do not discourage them... They are **strengthened** by the heat.

THOUGHT PROVOKING COMPOSITION.

A student said to the master, "Master, with all of your teaching my mind is like a fire with enough fuel to burn bright forever." To which the master replied, "Yes, you now have much fuel by which you might feed a fire. But even unlimited fuel cannot alone sustain the flame. For without fresh air, even the white hot will be snuffed. Come, let us breathe fresh air by pondering what is contained within each of the following pages." The potential master then turned the page

Time passes,

And although it is oblivious of me, it does not exclude me.

Within the circle, the second hand passes and we see a beginning. A new second, a new hour, a new life; marking events by the sweeping hand as it completes its round. The hand is oblivious of us, we who look to it for stability, we who search for meaning within its three hundred and sixty degree path. Never realizing the story being told with each second's pass.

But can't we hear it, see it?

Its story... Our story. Nothing hidden or complex, just the movement itself. Oblivious yes, yet forever an example for those who choose to see the truth.

Time passes,

And as always, the darkness becomes light.

Another day gone by,

Lost forever. Did you savor each

Moment, or did you suffer

Over inconsequential nonsense?

Saying you know you should change...

That's not quite enough.

Time passes,

And the pain has faded.

Why can we so easily perceive the onset of pain, yet be completely unaware of its absence?

Time passes,

And what was once a burning inspiration is now an afterthought.

Remember?

(The urgency, the anxiety; because you knew for sure what had to be done. The only way to insure your further existence! But you couldn't; you didn't. And yet, somehow, you survived.)
Don't forget it.

Time passes,

And even though we are together, we are both alone.

Why do we always desire more?

Are there limits to our expectations, or are we

Never fulfilled? If you can't buy what's missing, or fill

The empty space with the company of others, what do you need?

Time passes,

And I realize that the more I expect, the less I enjoy.

Most dreams taste better in the mind than they do on the palate.

Time passes,

And everything changes, except our needs.

Never does it cease to amaze me how

Every day is filled with the constant pursuit of

Every thing but that which is essential.

Desire only sounds like require. It is a vacuum

Time passes,

And the tides are still oblivious of me.

Is everything really anything at all?
I mean, we think we're big...
Maybe we're small.
The sky looks deep blue, but that's cause of light.
It'll be dark in an hour, that's cause it's night.
Thick grass is green, but only with water.
Brown leaves crunch, they got none so they oughta.
Relevant I'm told, relevant we all are,
I just hit two under, but who said five was par?
    Who's to say what's wrong, who's to say how hot,
Who's the judge, how come I'm not?
Who's to say that we're close, who's to say that we touched?
True, there's a feeling; but yet, it's not much.
Relevant I'm told, relevant we all are,
that can't be a plane, it's not moving. It must be a star.
    On my foot's a sneaker, on yours is a shoe,
we both ate what they came from - remember? It went "moo".
In mine I'll dump trash, in yours you'll sit and think.
If we don't wash our feet, I guarantee that they'll stink.
Relevant I'm told, relevant we all are,
Three blocks is so distant, let's just take my car.
    We control all we can; what we can't, we avoid.
Everything large we break down so it's small;
but infinite space to an ant, ain't much at all.

Time passes,

And all the cosmetic alteration in the world cannot change what we really are.

Realize that being in control of everything is not possible.

Everything is much more than you could ever be

Aware of. Think about it, what is not a potential

Learning experience? Realize that your action is of no

Importance to Natural Law, but don't despair;

The truth can only limit when it is unknown.

Your realization of this will set you free.

TIME PASSES,

AND A CAUSE STILL DOES NOT HAVE TO JUSTIFY AN EFFECT.

There will come a day when you can no longer

Have the luxury of making your own reality.

In time, certain rules you've ignored will present themselves

Effectively. This will force you to realize that they are

Very real. Real seems to be only what you make real, but when

Everything you've built comes crashing down around you, usually

Something must give. What will it be?

Time passes,

And the truth is still a matter of opinion. (To those who don't see it)

Through my eyes it's all the same, colors mean nothing
nor do their names.

Lest my eyes be an unfair judge, I seek all around me
and try not to rush.

I find much opinion unfounded by fact, words spoken quite
smoothly, no truth only tact.

So many sides; all want me to choose; they each pull real hard
yet claim nothing's to lose.

Pick a team and die for their cause, just don't have a problem;
they won't fight for yours.

Signs and rules where none should apply, heed their call
and they'll blind your **I**.

Time passes,

And too often our memories accord with our ability to re-arrange and
create where thefactsdon'tfitwell.

I don't think you're

Gonna be too happy,

Now or later, unless you

Organize thoughts and actions based on

Rational beliefs.

Anger, hate, fear and pain are all caused by

Not realizing the truth. Only the truth

Can set you free from delusion. And ironically

Enough, only by recognizing your delusion, can you find the truth.

Time passes

And somehow, that tiny blade of grass grows up through a crack in
the cement.

The only force stronger than imagination is the will to live it

Time passes,

And, as always, the light becomes darkness.

Helpless.

Helpless to safely guide my flight. Helpless to choose what's wrong from right. Like a moth I'm simply pulled toward bright.

But I'm no rabid dog, in fact I'm madder; I have to hide while I empty my bladder. Keep it to yourself, till you're out of reach, don't share it with the class unless it's just what we teach.

Yes, lost in thick fog yet onward we roll, with the illusion of control as all that comforts the soul.

Time passes,

And it becomes apparent that words are just that.

The biggest asset we have besides

Health is undoubtedly our ability to

Interpret what we affect, and what affects us.

Not utilizing this ability reduces all

Knowledge to the point of worthlessness.

Time passes,

And I realize that sight can cause a lack of vision.

Often, a blank page can say much more than one filled with words or pictures. The blank page has no designed perceptual cues. It lets our mind roam free, unattended

Time passes,

And I see that I don't always need what I think I need.

With each material gain our

Economy grows; so do our responsibilities.

At what point does our gain become a burden?

Lack of time exemplifies our values;

The rarer an item, the higher its price.

Health and peace of mind are not for sale.

Time passes,

And with its passing, I've learned to accept that some things will
always be out of my control.

As I ponder the word "own", I wonder: is it just coincidence that its letters, if transposed, spell "won" and "now", but never "later"?

Time passes,

And the wound is healing.

Alone.

Alone not because no one is with me, alone because I am a stranger to my self. I am the only possible constant in my universe, yet I am unstable.

One may often experience such feelings, yet choose to avoid them. What could be worse than facing the unknown, unbounded realm within? It poses many dangerous threats, such as being confronted by questions which require thought. Questions that, if honestly pursued, will make you realize there is, or could be, more to life than a job, a mate, a buzz, tv, and paying bills.

Time passes,

And that girl I loved, what was her name?

Ruby lips and eyes of fire, long tan legs that spell desire. Body shaped like an hour glass, that girl's too fine, can't let her pass. Blonde hair flowing with currents of air, words don't do justice cause words don't care. White teeth sparkle by the rays of the sun; they command more attention than a thief with a gun.

My feelings are true, they run so deep, this spot in my heart she'll always keep. Beauty so rare, so true, so real. I need the feel of... Whoa! Short and sweet with deep brown eyes, simply perfect calves and unreal thighs. Black hair shaped around a perfect face, brown skin like silk, she's worth the chase. I swear I'd quit breathing if I could just have a taste. She can't be real, from myself I'm told. Such a vision I need to love and hold.

My feelings are true, they run so deep, this spot in my heart she'll always keep. Beauty so rare, so true, so real. I need the feel of... Ooh! Perfection in the shape of a red haired angel, with curves so right they should warn of danger. Deep green eyes that stop me cold, fair skin so smooth I must be bold. Bold enough to make her mine; flesh so tight, so firm, so fine. She's too hot to handle, most crash and burn. But I'll have her forever, I won't waste my turn.

My feelings are true, they run so deep, this spot in my heart she'll always keep. Beauty so rare, so true, so real. I need the feel of... Oh man! Almond eyes make me stop on sight; until she's mine the world's not right. Skin that glows warm as the midday sun, every fiber of her being calls to me. I'm numb. Straight brown hair cascades down her back, with legs aflame she needs no name. I don't just want her; I need those lips of wine. I won't survive much longer if she's not mine........

Time passes,

And acceptance depends on the inability to avoid.

Rationalization is man's greatest tool.

It makes cold water hot and a wise man a fool.

Time passes,

And I realize that the majority of those times I ran, I could have walked.

To do what you must is to survive.

To do what you want is to live.

Time passes,

And I am still not qualified to judge anyone's worth, nor are they
qualified to judge mine.

How often am I close to you, without being anywhere near you?

How often do I make contact with you, without touching you?

How often do I touch without feeling?

How often do my eyes perceive without seeing?

How often do I speak without saying a word?

How often do I act, without action?

How often do I listen without hearing?

How often do I acknowledge, without understanding?

How often am I awake without being conscious?

Time passes,

And with its passing, all I've built will crumble.

Show me time. Where is it? What does it affect? How does it do that? You can't. It isn't. It doesn't. Time is only a representation of our realization of certain cycles which we observe and further divide in an attempt to maintain order in our lives.

Time does not wither the flower. Lack of vital nutrients, physical limitations and environmental stresses wither the flower.

Time passes,

And although they haven't really changed, many views look different.

We share "it don't", but it does. Spelled correct it says: I see.

Time passes,

And I realize that I don't necessarily get more out, just because I put more in.

What are your goals? Did you devise them

Or did someone else do that for you?

Realize the answer, then think about what you

Know and do.

Time passes,

And beauty still creates ugly.

What can't I do? I can't be you. I can't be the same, can't judge by a name. Nor do I want to. I can't feel good (though you think I should) about the current democracy. I can't laugh at the epitaph I know they'll surely write. Maybe I'm wrong, maybe it's night; a new day mere hours away. I can't believe that. I can't foresee robbing history of the times it shall repeat.

I can't believe an empty street while we use the fur but not the meat. I can't picture clean water or a tree, in the days our children might live to see. I can't imagine (or can I?) that your biggest care is not our air, but something else at which you stare.

What can I do? I can scare, when I turn to see you're looking at my hair. The length you say does not portray a man with social flair!

WAIT A SECOND

Beauty is... Appreciating everything for each nuance

which makes them what they are. Being able to accord positively

with immutable law, while doing what you prefer. Realizing

that strength comes from one, not many. Determination.

Wonder. An open ear. A helping hand. A word of encouragement. A smile.

Are you beautiful?

Time passes,

And these damned apple seeds still won't grow grapes.

Maturity is a constantly evolving state of acceptance.
Immaturity is the constant state of refusal.

Time passes,

And what was right, is still right.

Letters can't describe it, no matter how they're arranged.

Only by feeling it can you realize the

Very reason people live and die for it. Within

Everyone is the capacity to feel it. Maintenance is a virtue.

Time passes,

And the wound has healed.

Sometimes, all it takes to

Make a big difference

Is a tiny gesture. Don't be afraid,

Let go of your hardened stare and

Everyone else will do the same.

Time passes,

And what seemed to be moving too slow, now seems to have moved too fast.

Life is like seeing what's behind the window of a moving train. If you focus on it while it is still distant, you will be able to easily discern what you are looking at as it passes.

If you wait until it is in front of you, and then look, it's already too late.

Time passes,

And what was once an old bastard... Is me.

Remember when there was no grey?

It was all black and white. Play fair and

Good will prevail, respect all others,

Honesty is the best policy, brush your

Teeth. If you can still look yourself in the eye, don't sweat the dentures.

Time passes,

And all that I thought was beneath me is above me.

Theories and kingdoms are

Indefinite. Is change the only constant?

Moments pass with or without us, yet

Entire lives are wasted waiting for the right one.

THINK FISRT!

COMMENTARY.

After reciting perfectly all of the previous day's lesson, a student rejoiced and said rather smugly to a colleague, "What could I not accomplish by applying all of this combined knowledge?" Hearing the comment, the master replied, "Knowledge is the fuel by which a flame would torch the world. An honest search for understanding is the hearth which will contain and direct its heat."

Like so many other happenings, just because we are unaware of them or they are unaware of us, it doesn't mean that there isn't going to be an effect on us or them, as a result of the innumerable repercussions.

What are you oblivious of but do not exclude?

We long for stability and think we have it when we are able to put our life in "order". The more exacting our ability to measure and categorize the passing of our day (s), the more secure we feel (clocks help this tremendously). Sounds good, except for the fact that everything was not designed to fit into your neat little package, and no matter how hard you try, it won't.

The truth is not a matter of good or bad, it just is. You can accept truth and positively accord with it or you can fight it and suffer. Ultimately we are nothing more than what we think and do.

That's our story, just the movement itself. Suffer and complain - if you want.

TRUE TEACHING ENABLES AND ALLOWS:

If you teach someone the mechanics of walking yet restrict their steps,

have you taught them to walk or... to march?

If you teach someone to read but not how to question,

have you taught them to think or... to mimic?

Universally, if there is darkness there will be light.

Have you ever seen or heard of anything with only one side?

Individually, when we accept and accord positively with truth.

Without knowing everything, can you know anything?

Perspective is served.

A
L
M
O
S
T

It is said that knowing is half the battle, but that can't be so. How many people "know" that smoking is detrimental to their health, but do it anyway?

The more you do of anything the easier it gets. The less you do of anything the harder it becomes to do.

***This includes: addiction, worry, envy, hatred, not brushing one's teeth, etc...

"They" is anyone "we" are not, and "we" are "they" to "them".

Who are we, if they are us and we are them?

Imagine if hydrogen and oxygen were as intelligent and discriminating as us. We would all die of dehydration.

Unless, of course, you cling to it; let go of it and it will let go of you.

If not, it may become a comfortable routine.

How often do you complain about certain situations, yet continually recreate circumstances which cause the same results?

The key word is same. Same is familiar, and familiar is comforting to those who fear the unknown.

Do you fear the unknown, or are you actually more fearful of losing what is known, the self-made reality that supports your belief system?

What do you fear more, truth or loss of perceived control?

There is no nerve impulse for non-pain or non-pleasure. Our mind simply focuses on other stimuli. The key is to appreciate it.

If you appreciate something, what is the best way to insure its continuity?

* hint: it connects interrelationships to concepts.

Do we learn, or do we just pick new inspirations?

Do your goals still have the original basis of childhood desire, or has your awareness of self and interrelationships expanded?

If so, how?

Of course you survived.

Let's be honest: If it is not a matter of survival

- yours or theirs - can't it wait?

What happens if you keep opening the oven door to check on a soufflé?

What metabolic difference is there if you ingest a soufflé that fell, as opposed to one that rose perfectly?

What are you wasting when you worry?

What is more valuable than time, health, peace of mind and freedom?

So why waste them?

Even though we both agree that the sets of

letters below are identical in color, and agree

to call them "black", how do you know

that I don't see them as what you would call "pink"?

Aaaaa/bbbbb/ccccc/ddddd/eeeee/fffff/ggggg

How do you know that what we both agree are

"pink" letters, I don't see as "brown"?

Whether we like it or not, ultimately every experience is uniquely our own; no matter who it is shared with. This is the fundamental challenge of mankind. Human beings must see past what, on the surface, - to our senses - appear to be differences which justify separation.

W
A
N
T

    We always desire more because we want. There are no limits to our expectations as long as we have expectations, because want creates more wants; just as any action creates other actions.

    What you need is to gain accurate insight into your self; then you will realize that you already have enough.

Desire is like quicksand: soft, shifting, yields easily to pressure and tends to suck down any object moving on its surface.

How does one escape quicksand?

If you have no expectations, how can you be let down?

How can you have no expectations?

Realize that you cannot fully perceive of the whole

and therefore it is not in your best interest to

expect.

Perception wise, what would happen if you enjoy milk and you knowingly drink a glass of milk?

Perception wise, what would happen if you were thirsty and expected to ingest a mouthful of water, but instead drank a mouthful of milk?

How much appreciation of your actual life experience is wasted, wishing it were something other than what it is?

Milk tastes fine if you're open to the possibility of drinking milk. The same goes for water; but neither is "good" if you are expecting the other.

Too often our dreams and desires are based on un-realistic beliefs.

So even if we get what we think we want, it rarely turns out to be

what we expected.

Are you aware of all the interrelationships involved in the coming to fruition of your fantasies?

You're not even aware of all the interrelationships involved in the actuality of you wiping your ass and flushing the toilet.

What are your needs?

Anything not related directly to your well-being (as it relates to natural environmental homeostasis) is not a need. This is the starting point of much confusion. It begins when we are very young and is constantly negatively reinforced until we are lowered into the ground in our highly polished, brass accented, velvet lined coffins.

How do you spell want?

- double you ant -

What does that say?

Yes, the word want actually mocks us. It laughs at our fruitless struggles and at the confusion which ensues as we attempt to satiate misunderstood desire. It says, while laughing: "Try, give it your all - double, you ant! Hah, hah, hah!" (Personally I find the "HA, ha, ha!" to be nails-scratching-chalkboard-like, but it does drive the point home)

Double, triple, whatever number you desire, how does this impact your essential being?

N
E
E
D

Isn't it incredible that people spend their whole lives expending energy in search of, and worrying about, that which is not essential to their actual well-being? (Wants disguised as needs) They believe that such pursuits are needed to achieve happiness; but they only lead to confusion and a sense of emptiness.

How else does "want" mock us?

It mocks us by appearing to aid in multiplication (the gathering of goods) but it knows that our attempts at multiplication are really subtraction... Of self. Think about it: "desire", "de" = reversal or undoing, reduction. Disparagement; "sire" = the father, to father. What is happening when we desire?

We are dismantling what we are, by cutting off our connection to the Source. When we cut off our connection to the Source - our self - we give others the ability to sire our values and perspective, which we then mistakenly believe to be the Source. We disempower ourselves, creating a vacuum within.

If you transpose the letters in "need", you have "Eden".

Why? Because if you stick to your needs, you won't castrate paradise.

No matter how important our endeavors appear to be, they are not.

No matter what, no matter who, the tides could not care less. It is not about us. It is, regardless of us.

Feeling small? Good.

Realize and accord positively with your place in the scheme of things.

But aren't we the self-proclaimed pinnacle of evolution?

What about control?

Everything is related, everything has an explanation. But making up our own rules based on unfounded conclusions (usually done in an attempt to give ourselves - as a species and individually - more importance than we deserve; in an attempt to give meaning to a relatively short, often painful existence) can only compound the confusion we were trying to replace.

Within the realm of duality, if something appears unimportant or insignificant, it is simply because of your limited awareness.

Realize that insignificance is a man-made invention. It was originally used to help differentiate between immediate necessity and what could wait. It later evolved, helping elevate us to our current status as the pinnacle of evolution, and it is still used to keep us there, their and they're. "It serves me in no way and its existence is of no consequence to me. It is insignificant".

By comparing ourselves and our endeavors to all of these seemingly unimportant entities and events - which can only speak for themselves in as much as we can make sense of them through our limited, projecting perspective - what else could we, in all of our ignorance, be, but important?

Thank goodness I didn't forget the "r" in important. Don't ever forget the "r". It makes you right. If you're not right, you're impotent.

No matter how you decorate it, or refer to it, the outhouse is where you shit. Did I say shit? Sorry, I meant poo poo.

When we color what we are with words that seem "less harsh", we only invite disaster. By using the "rest room" when animals don't even use a toilet, we - in our imagination - levitate to a higher level of decency than those vile creatures without shame. But think about how this affects us when certain functions of homeostasis decide to say hello: embarrassment because of natural bodily function. How absurd is it that our imaginary virtue causes us to be ashamed of what we are, and must be?

Bowel movements, boogers, and baldness; pimples, wrinkles, gray hair, and dandruff; height, body type, and even death; our attempts to shun them are what causes any problems associated with them.

Why do we shun? Because we fear. Why do we fear? Because we are ignorant. Why are we ignorant? Because we shun.

R
E
A
L
I
T
Y

   If circumstances are infinite and ever changing, how can a finite
being with finite awareness who is affected by change, control
circumstance?
   Realizing that you are of no importance to something that is and
must be of great importance to you, should not cause despair; it should
simply cause you to re-evaluate and, if necessary, re-define your values
and perspectives. Truth is what we must establish our parameters by.
Non-awareness of truth is what limits us, because we are most apt to
fail if we don't follow the rules that apply to us. Making up our own
rules regardless of truth, in attempts to give more importance to our
lives, is a sure way to cause untold problems.
   When you realize who and what you are (your nature), and that
who and what you are is O.K. (you will realize this when you realize
your nature - beyond character*), and you rejoice in it, you will be free.

*** Character is simply the projection of acquired perspectives. Most
acquired perspectives mask our nature and the nature of most, if not all,
that we experience.

Let go of all you've been taught.

Observe without your senses.

Search the dark unknown places

That you claim as yourself.

Doing whatever you want, regardless or unaware of the consequences, is a sure way to? Cause problems! You may appear to get away with it, but someone will eventually suffer.

Usually, what goes wrong is what someone appeared to get away with coming to fruition. Nothing just happens.

Nothing just happens. What just ends?

Does anything really end, or does it all just blend?

T
H
I
E
V
E
S

How does that song go?

The knee bone's connected to the thigh bone; the thigh bone's connected to the hip bone, etc... That idea applies to everyone and everything. Clear cut forest and there will be - to say the least - floods. Kill off the bottom of the food chain and the top will suffer. Smoke and your body will fail you. Lie to people and you will eventually lose their trust. Ignore your self and your self will stagnate and disappear.

The strongest prayer is correct action.

Simply convincing yourself, and even others, of something does not always work. Sometimes it's enough, but have you ever heard of a cop wearing a bulletproof vest made only of ring spun cotton?

If you experienced undifferentiated consciousness

and then attempted to speak about your experience,

who would be able to properly interpret your explanation?

Who would believe you?

Would that invalidate your experience?

We must each search for truth, because those who like to tell us about it usually have something to gain in us following their version. Consequently, their gain is usually our loss. Our loss is usually our accurate perception of the facts, which usually results in our loss of self and freedom.

I want to fly,
But I have no wings.

I want to save those drowning,
But I can't swim.

I want to carry the world,
But I can barely stand.

I want to heal the sick,
But I've got a cold.

I want to seek what's right,
But I have no map.

I want to demand justice,
But that would be criminal.

I want to sing the gospel,
But I have no voice.

I want to spread the light,
But I'm in the dark.

I want to free the captive,
But I'm imprisoned.

I want to tear down the wall,
But there are so many bricks
I don't know where to start.

We can learn only from the past

(however brief the interlude).

So how can ignoring and disguising it

possibly benefit us?

Never be ashamed of what you did, only of what you are doing.

(If it's not right and you see why)

I
G
N
O
R
A
N
C
E

Not until we look inside ourselves and realize that it is us – our misconceptions, which are continually reinforced through many social mediums and our own rationalization - can we begin to see things as they are.

My mind is a magnifying glass. Whatever

It focuses on is expanded, yet if it is

Not angled correctly it will completely

Distort the image it is supposed to clarify.

Certainly the grass doesn't muscle its way through the cement, how does it do it?

Constancy to purpose? Obviously. But what purpose?

Do birds and airplanes conquer the laws of physics?

Imagine freedom. Imagination can engender freedom.

If freedom is measurable by the length of our chains, what is

the act of breaking those chains worth?

Until you try, you can have no idea of the results that even ten
minutes a day, every day, of anything, can make over time.

How many links in your chain are there only because of attempts to "accomplish" and "achieve", in order to live what you have been taught is the "good life"?

How many of those who taught you the "good life" live (d) a truly fulfilling existence?

Look at the depth, not the surface. Light from the surface is only an illusion. The surface has no light of its own. It is simply reflecting light from elsewhere. Like a diamond.

Universally, of course, there must be balance.

Individually, if we don't cultivate the light within us (our self) it will appear quite dim; causing us to seek artificial light from other sources.

How many hours a day do you spend illuminating your path with artificial light?

How many hours a day do you spend cultivating the light within?

If you're not doing one, you're doing the other.

"Indecent exposure" really sums up our warped sense of value. How is it possible that by simply being in our natural physical state, we could be indecent? Yet, wrapped in the fur of animals killed only for their fur, we are not merely decent, but stately. Wearing sneakers and clothing made by people working under conditions we would never want our own children to suffer - while being paid less per hour than one minute's worth of our legal minimum wage - is not merely decent, but is actually quite fashionable. Creating garbage that we send to other places in attempts to ignore the fact that our lifestyle causes environmental destruction is not only perfectly decent, but is considered smart thinking. The list of "decencies" is much too long for me to document. What does this tell you about the people whose values cause the creation of our laws, fashions, and teaching curriculum?

No wonder so many people feel helpless in so many ways. They are not crazed animals; they are products of their environment. Having to discard their nature at a young age, because exploration of self has been deemed socially unacceptable (there is no "profit" in it), is the reason people feel lost and helpless. Being "fashionable" or dyeing your hair green and getting tattooed or pierced are not expressions of what you really are; these are expressions of your current perspectives, which arise from not having awareness of self. These acts are a veneer and are used as a substitute for actual familiarity with one's self. When you gain awareness of what you really are, you don't need any props to show the world or to entertain yourself.

Not teaching people to discover *what* they are (the fine print), but rather to merely identify *who* they are (the headline) by what they wear, own, or have achieved - when even "achievement" is only recognized if it is in regard to socially accredited endeavors, (which usually require the abandonment of individual cultivation in an effort to fit into an unnatural framework of rules which contradict the forces by which we are governed) is the reason we are strangers to our selves; grasping the illusions presented to us. Control?

Shame rhymes with same and claim because only when it is claimed that we should be the same, can we feel shame. Name rhymes with shame, same, and claim because only when we name, can we claim what should be the same; creating shame. Tame rhymes with shame, same, claim and name because when we are taught to claim, by using names, to be the same and thus feel shame, we find our selves lacking, insipid (dull, uninteresting); which causes us to look elsewhere for fulfillment.

Lame and maim also rhyme with shame, same, claim, name, and tame; because the claim to be the same, created by name, which causes us to feel shame, so we'll become tame, maims us - crippling the growth and abilities of our self, enabling others to more easily govern us. Game also rhymes with shame, same, claim, name, tame, lame, and maim because it can not only mean an object of ridicule or scorn - and when hunting, isn't anything not tame, game? But it means lame, crooked; not to mention that it is also because games claims are named arbitrarily. Is it just coincidence that game also means a vocation or business, especially a competitive one?

Do you see the dame whence the flame of blame and fame are framed, came?

Take aim.

***(dame=woman=paramour=adulterous=adulterate)

Words are simply vehicles for the transmission of concepts. Like packages and containers, what good are they unless they contain something of value? And of what value is a transmission if the receiver is unable to open the package?

What good is an unopened can of food to a dog?

And yet... by way of the prudent usage of words, such as prudent, we can each perceive of the importance of having an accurate awareness of those funda*mental* constructs which enable us to experience what we call "time" and "space" - and to have a conscious, accurate awareness of the difference between them.

Since we're on the subject, do you personally believe that either time or space is directly dependent upon the other?

Why exactly do you believe that?

Do you think that both the form and substance of your explanation are based upon sound logic?

Why exactly do you think that?

Are you aware of the fact that your properly structured usage of the proper words is one of the keys to your being able to offer others such an explanation?

What do you think some of the other keys might be?

Are you aware of the fact that their properly structured usage of the proper words is one of the keys to others being able to properly interpret your explanation?

What do you think some of the other keys might be?

T
H
I
N
K

The biggest asset we have besides

Health is undoubtedly our ability to recognize

Interrelationships. However limited,

Not utilizing this ability reduces all

Knowledge to the point of worthlessness.

Wisdom is the bridge that connects knowledge to understanding. It is constructed only through the constant evolution of applied learning.

Should our vision be limited to what our eyes perceive? When we see, we are able to recognize and become familiar. Recognition and familiarity enable people to believe that they know. Believing that they know causes people to feel as though they understand. When people assume that they understand, they no longer take the time to see things as they really are.

Isn't it funny that the only way to know exactly what we look like is

through what is called "Reflection"?

By any other method, what we are seeing will be backward.

Everything is what it is, regardless of what we perceive and then

believe.

Or

Don't perceive and can't believe

Boundaries, such as our senses for instance, limit our potential mental experience. Because they deal with and judge only by the quantifiable, they restrict our ability to experience and realize all that is beyond such measurement. Just because our senses cannot perceive of a concept, does that mean there can be no such concept?

The boundaries are created by our desire to define.

What happens when we define?

To de-fine is to "**de**" (reversal or undoing. Removal. Degration, reduction. Disparagement.) "**fine**" (of superior quality. Most enjoyable. Having no clouds; clear.).

We - in our imagination - separate and judge what is inseparable.

What happens if you judge what is incomplete, while basing all judgement on the belief that what you are judging is complete?

When we define we make clouds where there were none. We obscure what we were trying to uncover.

Since we are unaware of this, we are also unaware that our belief in the actuality of everything we see and do that is based upon the resulting misconception is illusion.

This illusion can potentially encompass one's entire life.

Remember, you can call me what you want, but I will remain what I am.

We must attempt to gain an accurate awareness of the nature of our existence, in order to recognize that wants are not needs. Or we will forever be slaves to our - and perhaps more importantly, others - whims and desires. Can you say diamond? Two month's salary?!

***Others: teachers, parents, peers, government, automakers, clothing designers, sneaker manufacturers, fast food chains, beverage companies, etc......

<u>Stop</u> acquiring. <u>Start</u> inquiring

How can we do that?
(check one)

A) - by observing without defining.

B) - through manipulation

***Defile and define are listed sequentially in the dictionary. It's almost as if defile is a warning, or portent, of what will happen if we define.

W
E
A
L
T
H

What is enough? (Of anything) Equilibrium. Balance. The fine line between too little and too much. Just as it is what's not between two walls which allows us to occupy such space, it is what's not happening in our life at any given time which allows us to reflect upon and gain an accurate awareness of what *has* happened – which then allows us to enjoy what *is* happening. If we don't stop, everything just blends into one fast moving mess. Before we know it, whatever was "supposed" to serve us we now serve. Working extra hours and struggling for what is "supposed" to make our lives easier; routinely allowing peripheral events to become bigger than our selves.

If, as our values indicate, that which is in shortest supply holds the highest value, and we strive to possess that which holds the highest value, shouldn't we expend our energies on health and tranquility? Or are we so misled that we can appreciate only what is tangible?

How often do you sacrifice principle in attempts to attain or become principal?

I will ask this again: if circumstances are infinite and ever changing,

how can a finite being with finite awareness who is affected by

circumstance control circumstance?

Granted, having knowledge of certain physical laws can enable us to control certain physical processes, such as keeping a car on the road, a ball in our hand, or creating a physical structure (house, car, bridge etc...); but even that actual control can be limited by the innumerable outside forces with which we co-exist.

Trying to control is the best way to lose control. What do we lose control of when we try to control? Our ability to accord positively with the laws that govern us. How? We become consumed with the notion that we must cause events to happen in a certain way. We become lost in judgement. This creates the birth of our own reality, a.k.a. perspective. Control is a function that arises from the belief that we are able to judge which outcome is best; which could only come from the belief (conscious or unconscious) that we understand the entire process of the infinite reality in which we are included.

So what is the only way to control?

Be in positive accord with the interplay of elemental energy, as such interplay relates to that which you seek to accomplish.

35a

Yes, we can win or even earn physical titles and we can often retain them for periods of time. But what's to stop events from occurring which will take these items away from us? The forces of the universe are not impressed by brick walls and guns. Only beliefs/ideas which are in positive accord with truth can be retained regardless of circumstance. Retained, not owned. How can you own that which is the intangible universal foundation of what is tangible?

Whatever is, is. To name and say that we "own" or "won" something, or to refer to - as with "now", is simply an attempt to grasp (seize, control); but when we grasp, we weaken our selves.

We try to grasp because we believe it is the only way to achieve our desired ends. But personal fulfillment and accurate orientation are not dependent upon the ability to substantiate. As a matter of fact, the "proof" or "evidence" we present inhibits our success because we forget that what we present is actually but a representation (like our reflection in a mirror) and we come to believe that it is the actual truth.

Think about it. Even the word "now" is an attempt to measure, so as to enable representation of our concept of time; which is but another representation. We commonly mistake so many representations for the genuine article that we have come to see the tool as the purpose. This is because the fact that they were originally tools meant to strengthen us has been concealed and the concealment has been reinforced for many centuries. How? Through our usage of the misrepresentations presented to us by those who have and those who continue to shape common opinion and conduct. This has caused us to become a tool for the new purpose (which was originally the tool).

Unfortunately, only when we are able to substantiate something do we believe it to be real and of any value. And only can it be taken from us.

Physically, the pain will fade and the wound will heal; but they will both recur continuously unless we learn to avoid their cause. Mentally they can heal only when we learn to avoid their cause.

"Misconception"!

"Mis" = failure. "Conception" = a beginning, start. A concept, plan, or thought.

The problem is not that you misread the rule book. The problem is that the authors of the rule book didn't understand the actuality of what they were writing about. Or perhaps your being lost was a part of their plan?

Now go back to the start and see just how far off course you are.

Am I the only possible constant in "my universe"? Granted, since I am directly affected when I change, I can attain an informed awareness of those changes - if I was aware of my intrinsic-self prior to such change. If, on the other hand, I am not aware of my intrinsic-self, I will continuously be lost. So, instead of the misinformed egocentric phrase "my universe", how about "From my limited vantage point (which is inclusive of my being oblivious to the changes in my beliefs that got me to this vantage point), my current beliefs are the only possible constant I can perceive of..."

We easily get stuck in our limited, limiting perspectives. Yet, unlike attics and closets, our intrinsic-self (i.e., unchanging truth) cannot be forever avoided. Obviously those beliefs which we try to avoid are associated with some manner of discomfort; but, ironically, it is only because we try to avoid them. Avoidance consumes much more time and energy than would be necessary to properly come to terms with the situation or situations we try to avoid in the first place.

Know this:

In this realm of near infinite possibility,

it is no wonder one often portrays the fool.

Know this too:

It is only after subsequent performances are played

on the same stage, that we truly assume the role.

Holding on means you think you know the future. Why else would you hold on? When we are willing to let go of the misconception that we know what is best, and that events are mysteriously designed to turn out in what we believe to be our favor, we can let go of anyone or anything.

Who, what, where, why, when and how, are the six most potentially dangerous words in the English language. Each one is taken to be definitive of whatever answer one might seek; yet, unless their outer surface is penetrated, they all - collectively and individually - explain only the perceivable "parts" of what is actually a singular event which has been unfolding since the genesis of creation.

Oh no! She's gone... Oh wow, it's a good thing she's gone or I wouldn't have met this one.

Oh no! She's gone... Oh wow, it's a good thing she's gone or I wouldn't have met this one.

Oh no! She's gone... Oh wow, it's a good thing she's gone or I wouldn't have met this one.

Oh no! She's gone... Oh wow, it's a good thing she's gone or I wouldn't have met this one.

The names and places will vary, but the dilemma will not; until we change. Ironically, it seems like the one thing we can come closest to understanding is that we cannot actually understand. Remember: what appears to be bad can turn out to be good; and what appears to be good can turn out to be bad.

Cancel all your plans, there are

Happenings occurring that will

Alter your entire perspective - knowing

Nothing going in, knowing even less going out -

Can we avoid them or will any such

Efforts actually cause their fruition?

Only when we cannot ignore that which does not fit

into our existing perspective does our perspective expand.

What is your perspective based on?

It is based upon what you think you understand.

What do you understand?

Rationalization is what we use to avoid changes in our perspective. But what happens if, after years of avoidance, there is an inability to avoid?

It makes no difference to the dentist whether you go every six months or not. But the longer you wait, the more painful (physically and monetarily) it will be. This is applicable to every aspect of your life.

RATIONALE CHECKLIST

Why is it always today?

Why am I always here?

Why am I never there?

Who are they?

Who am I ?

What am I?

What is?

What is real?

What constitutes good?

Where is now?

When is now?

When is later?

Why not?

Who says?

Because of the running, did you enjoy more or gain peace of mind? When you see that the majority of your actions have been counterproductive to the growth of your self-awareness, and you realize that you cannot foresee the effects of your actions, why would you rush them?

Confusion

"Con" = against. "Fusion" = union.

What union?

The union of all that is; the whole.

Confusion is - as a result of no "double you" - the hole.

When we cause separation through our misconception we go against

what is in essence a unified whole.

Shouldn't there be a picture of a new car under that statement? Or at least the logo of some company, to reinforce that they have what you want?

According to that statement, if you want it you actually need it. Because if you don't get what you want you're not living; you're only surviving. And we don't survive life to the fullest; we live life to the fullest.

The message is subtle and it is everywhere.

If doing what you must is to survive and doing what you want is to live, but wanting is detrimental to your ability to accord positively with natural environmental homeostasis, and simply surviving is not living, what are you to do?

Re-define your basis for differentiation. Don't cause the whole to become a hole.

Upon what criteria am I able to judge?

How do I know what functions are being carried out in the vast scheme of existence by this person?

If I am aware of this person, it is myself whom I must evaluate in relation to what I perceive. I must decide what is best for me based upon my beliefs. I cannot judge what is best for the other person because I am only able to see from my extremely limited view. Furthermore, I'm not even sure that what I see and choose is best for me, and I see me better than I can see anyone else.

We only perceive things as strange because of our limited awareness. Everything would make perfect sense if we could see the entire picture.

How often are we physically close to one another, while mentally or spiritually distant?

How often are we mentally or spiritually close to one another, while physically distant?

How often do we make actual physical contact, without mental or spiritual affect?

How often do we mentally or spiritually affect, without physical contact?

How often do we mentally or spiritually affect, without consideration or care?

How often do we physically touch without clouding our realization of what is really there, with our assumptions of what should be there?

How often do our eyes perceive but a fraction of what is within their spectrum?

How often do we make statements simply by our action?

How often do our ears perceive without having realized the actuality of what was said, whether or not it was intended to be heard?

How often do we claim to have understanding, without having an actual awareness of what is involved?

How often are we not sleeping, yet at the same time, quite unaware of what we have an effect on, and what it is that is affecting us?

I can't help but think of a story I was told by an acquaintance: Alana told me that when she was in the second grade and the class was making holiday decorations, the teacher assumed that, because of her last name, she should make a menorah. "But," Alana told her, "my mommy is Catholic." So the teacher said, "Make a Christmas tree." "But," said Alana, "my daddy is Jewish." So then the teacher asked, "Well, do you go to temple or church?" When Alana answered "Neither.", the teacher replied, "Then go sit in the corner and read a book." So she went and sat next to the Indian kid in the corner.

"It flies and has a beak, it must be a bird".

Physically speaking, yes. But it is not time that will cause the deterioration. Mentally and spiritually, that which is in positive accord with truth will not deteriorate. Truth is the essence of all that is. How can that which is universally intrinsic end?

As much as we might try, we cannot fashion truth. Truth is not fashionable.

Yet if it were - socially speaking - we wouldn't have to try.

Slaves of our own invention, how typical.

Without verbal ability we would still be subject to the effects of the cycles upon which we base our measurements, but the extent to which we entangle our lives would be greatly reduced. Picture how much more efficiently cats and dogs could budget their time, and how vastly their productivity would increase, if only they could standardize and communicate such discoveries. Absurd isn't it?

What does the word "Time" say?

It says "ti - me". It can tie me in or it can tie me up. The choice is mine. Time was originally utilized as a way to accord positively with environmental homeostasis, by enabling us to have certain human endeavors coincide with natural function. High and low tide, for instance; sunrise and sunset, etc... Somewhere along the way though, the function of time became like a flame out of control (ironic, because it was our finely tuned "control" that allowed it to happen), and instead of warming us as planned, it destroyed everything it was supposed to enhance.

Through the combined use of time and other man made items meant to enhance our natural experience, we, as a society became tied up. And the rope gets tighter with each tic of the clock. Are you tied in or tied up?

They didn't change, I did. Our perspective evolves over time, usually quite subtly. That music you once despised, but now enjoy, it didn't change one note. The issues involved between parent and child don't change either, you do.

Look back. Remember all those burning inspirations you once had.

Don't they seem funny now?

What makes you think the ones you have now

will appear any different?

We share the misconception that it doesn't (it can be anything), but in actuality it does. When we view it correctly (spelled correct), it will make sense to us (I see). Common opinion is not necessarily correct. We must each look for the facts from as many angles as possible and take into account that there are probably many, many more angles involved than we are aware of at this particular time, and possibly ever will be. We must always use sound logic to fully examine calls for "pragmatism". A sober view of history shows us that pretty much whatever our leaders are selling today as "practical" will be re-branded tomorrow as the problem which the next "practical solution" is sure to fix.

And don't forget that germ theory was once laughed at by doctors. There were "experts" who once believed that man was physiologically incapable of running a mile in less than four minutes. What does this tell us? Common theories on innumerable subjects are constantly changing, simply because more of what is actually involved becomes uncovered. The facts don't change; our perception of them does.

Do they hide from us, or is it we who hide from them?

Dis - cover. Think about what this says: when we discover things, rarely must we do anything more than expand our ability to perceive what is plainly evident. It is our perspective obscuring our perception, through belief in false concepts, which restricts our awareness.

It is we who must be dis - covered. Only when you *dis* - cover what you are, are you able to see anything else for what it is.

Why would you, if what you are doing is contrary to the inherent nature

of what you are dealing with?

The early bird catching the worm is a thousand-page book, yet only the last sentence of the last page details the actual capture of the worm. Do you think that by simply showing up early, the bird is handed the worm? The early bird that gets the worm is not the bird who wakes up early and flies off in search of willing worms. The early bird that gets the worm is the bird who diligently prepares far in advance of the heralded attempt, by studying intimate details of the worm that the worm is not even aware of. So when finally the studious bird sets off in its attempt to get the worm, it needn't be concerned about the time of day; but rather, the size of its basket.

W
O
R
K

How did you come to value what you value?

It takes effort to uphold our values, whether it be through mental conditioning or physical labor. If we don't consider why we do what we do, how can we realize whether what we do is a beneficial or harmful expenditure of energy?

How much of what you believe and do did you, after searching and pondering, actually decide on?

When we move into a house, do we necessarily leave the same paint on the walls as the people who we bought the house from?

Why not?

When we make decisions based on unfounded opinion, the perception of truth is distorted and lines which don't belong are drawn.

Did you notice that "Beautiful" is spelled with only one "l"? That's not quite full. Coincidence? Yes. Inconsequential? I think not. Let me ask, are who and what we call "Beautiful" full of beauty, or have we, in effect, allowed others to eliminate the cause from effect in their attempts to legitimize and profit - at our expense - from their own agenda?

How can we base our values on what is fashionable, when fashion is based on a whim? What is beautiful today may be ugly tomorrow. The same people who told you how great their '95 model was - when they were trying to get rid of them - now tell you that the '95 is really outdated junk, you need the new '98.

We implode because of our lack of awareness of truth.

We implode through our attempts to expand upon what caused our initial implosion.

We implode at an exponential rate as we continue to act on our misconceptions.

We implode, eventually causing a catastrophic chain reaction of explosions.

We explode because of the accumulated pressure of our implosion.

We explode, further obscuring awareness of truth with our fallout.

We explode and the released pressure is so great that it causes those affected to implode.

Slow down, take a step back. Don't get pulled into the confusion. Those who profit from our confusion - almost everyone with something to sell - want to keep our heads spinning constantly; because if we slow down and think, we'll realize that they are full of shit.

Dare to scratch the surface.

You'll find that most claims are simply

veneer.

Since we were on the subject, I figured I'd advertise my not for profit model of beauty: appreciating everything for each nuance which makes them what they are means not being clouded by perspectives that distort our perception. If your beliefs are not in positive accordance with immutable law, the choices you make will verbally and physically cause problems to be set in motion - by way of negative accord - whose cause, and even existence, you may not ever be aware of. Realizing that strength comes from one, not many, is realizing that any structure is only as strong as its weakest link. This is not limited to the physical; it applies also to our beliefs. If there is not strength in one, how can there be strength in many?

Determination is being resolute in your convictions, regardless of the flavor of the day. Again, this is advised only when your beliefs are in positive accordance with immutable law. Wonder is a conscious awareness of the world being much larger and more purposefully constructed than we had imagined. And so, in regard to increasing the frequency of its occurrence and its duration, and the benefits that they impart, such experience is merely dependent upon our willingness to expand our perspectives. An open ear is the ability to listen to others. Only by listening can we realize if there is merit in what others say. Don't ever underestimate anyone. You never know who will say what may turn out, after careful consideration, to be an important different perspective. A helping hand is the ability to see beyond what may appear singular (e.g., "me", "you"), through at least some awareness of what is common. Let us cultivate this awareness. Words of encouragement often shed light into what would otherwise be confusing, debilitating darkness; but they are not necessarily advice concerning specific situations. Remember your limitations. A smile is an invitation to expand the boundaries of the personal toward some form of consciously shared existence; whether it be only for acknowledgement to the respectful existence of the other, or to fraternize. What are you full of?

If not ingested, even food for thought will go bad.

Pretty nifty phrase, right? Well, this is another example of words falsely representing concepts. The above statement looks and sounds good; but upon further inspection we see that, in a subtle way, this statement will negatively alter the perception of truth. It is telling us that truth and attempts at finding it are subject to expiration; when in actuality, these foods never go bad (though eventually their usefulness in what are commonly referred to as "particular situations" may expire)..
DARE TO SCRATCH THE SURFACE!

Alchemists have yet to turn copper to gold! Will you?

Is this a dream? Have I entered a

seem through which truth split;

a parallax universe where

many believe what they

cannot conceive, thrust

at conception toward

another's deception?

I've seen insects and birds kill themselves by repeatedly smashing into windows, and dogs who'll keep running full speed to the end of their rope. The measure of a man is not how many times he gets up after being knocked down, but what he thinks of and does between attempts.

The term "paying attention" is a misnomer.
Lack of attention is what costs us.

If it is no longer right, it never was right.

It may have conveniently fit. It may have worked perfectly within its parameters. It may have served its purpose for that time. But that doesn't mean that it was ever right.

Asbestos, lead paint, pesticides, deforestation, landfills, ocean dumping, burning of fossil fuels, animal testing, slavery, and certain inter-personal relationships; for example.

You said your love came for free, but that just can't be true. Take a look at the fortune my heart spent on you. I won't say you're a thief, I won't say you used me, but with all the loving I gave, I almost did lose me. One thing I learned, though it took pain to see, is, - while I'm lost in you, there ain't no me.

We're both searching for an answer, it's one that's plain as day to see. Yeah, problem is mine's not inside you, and babe yours ain't inside of me. No babe, yours ain't inside of me.

The only love that comes free is one that's our own, it's one that we find, never one that we're shown. Time might be my doorway, but you're not the key; 'cause what opens that lock must be inside me. If I can't stand on my own, I'll just be leaning on you. And that wouldn't be fair, love wouldn't be true.

L
O
V
E

    Love. Letters can't describe it no matter how they're arranged, because love is acceptance. Acceptance does not define; it simply accords with what is. Letters' entire basis of existence is to define. The exact nature of love is the exact opposite of letters. Trying to appreciate love through definition is like trying to increase a flame with water.

    Which is why only by feeling it, can you realize the very reason people live and die for it. How could I describe the color "turquoise" to someone who has never seen? It must be experienced. The experience is the beauty. Within everyone is the capacity to feel it, to accept. We must all simply let go of what we "know", realizing that it clouds what is actually in front of us. Maintenance is a virtue because if we don't maintain these realizations, we'll get pulled right back into the confusion.

What is the highest form or ideal of love? Unconditional love.

What is the only way to love unconditionally?

Let's review the first paragraph of the last page, specifically, "the exact nature of love is the exact opposite of letters'. Trying to appreciate love through definition is like trying to increase a flame with water". This statement is fine as long as we don't mistake scrutinization for definition or vice versa; but if we do, we will believe love is a mystical occurrence that operates outside the laws which govern everything else. We will believe that love is bigger than we are and we will never be aware of why we are loving and being loved; we will never question why it comes and goes or what we can do about it.

The act of loving is the act of acceptance; and, as with any act, a description cannot be substituted for actual experience. But scrutinization of the concept of love doesn't take anything away from the act. On the contrary, it enhances not only our ability to experience the act, but also to appreciate the experience. This is like going to a "foreign" movie and being able to speak the language (as opposed to having no idea of what is being said). You'll get much more out of the movie. Love is not a mystical emanation without structure. Like everything else, love has structure. And, as with everything else, ignoring the actuality of that structure and imagining it to be something else, based on misguided desire with a dash of grey area and some luck sprinkled on, is only a recipe for disaster.

Yes, the act of love is always acceptance; but so too is the origin of any supposed form of love (including what is known as "lust"; although this is a much narrower form). Why do we love others? Trust, respect, common bond (could be anything: values, activities etc...), admiration, security, succinct communication (not necessarily verbal). And yet, the concepts represented by those words are like so many musical instruments in a symphony or spices in a meal: you don't realize they're there until they're not. As commonly conceived, the title "love", like so many other titles which represent plural aspects of our consciousness, is translucence (e.g., like, dislike, comfortable, uncomfortable, perception, perspective, beauty, ugly, etc...).

In this respect, the word "love" is not unlike the word "luck"; in that it is really but a word representing a conceptual crutch ("luck" is our way of admitting our limitations without having to recognize them). The term "love" is used to put an amalgamation of concepts perceived in a sensory manner together - without consciously scrutinizing how and why the many aspects of this concert of concepts actually affects us. Our minds create concepts, often unbeknown to us, anytime there is any perception. Each concept when accessed (consciously or unconsciously) always causes a potentially perceptible feeling (potentially, because it can occur very easily without our being aware of it).

If scrutinized, the feelings of "love" that we perceive will give way to the conceptual basis upon which they are formed. If scrutinized, this conceptual basis will give way to the how and why that it was formed. When stripped of its unconscious, sensory based shell, the essential aspects constituting what we call "love" will be exposed. Upon examination of their essential aspects, we will find their common conceptual essence: Acceptance.

60a

But how do we prevent new or recurring injury?

Through constant positive reinforcement of the truth we have independently realized.

Everyone knows when they have it bad,

how many are aware of when they have it good?

S
M
I
L
E

Try it, it's accepted in more places than your credit card!

"Smile" = "s" - "mile". "S" = small. "Mile"= a unit of length. Measurement of distance. Why? Because when we smile, we shorten the distance between each other through acknowledgement. We are obviously aware of each other when eye contact is made, but that alone does not bring us any closer to one another. A smile brings us closer because, without words, it says many things depending on the situation. Through a smile we can agree, we can laugh silently; we can show interest, happiness, and acceptance. Through our smile we can invite others, without fear of rejection and without imposition, into a shared existence. Without words, through this shared existence, we can participate in the brotherhood of mankind. And through our smile we can recite silently, in unison, the highest ideal and oath of our brotherhood: Do not do unto others that which you would not have them do unto you.

A healthy dose of perspective.

What is slow?

What is fast?

Can't slow be   fast?

Can't fast be s - l - o - w ?

I've never heard of a "slow" day that wasn't faster than a forty hour work week that "flew by!"

For someone who has lived only five years, one hour is the equivalent of ten hours to a fifty year old. So a three hour car ride for that child is the equivalent of thirty hours straight, in a car, to a fifty year old. Just thinking about it makes my legs cramp, and my bladder feel full.

Did you make any preparations, or were you too busy?

Or were you too busy making preparations? This is when we see if we've maintained a proper balance. If all we did was look to the future, we missed the present (a dual meaning: if we look only ahead, we miss what is currently around us and thus *the* present cannot become *a* present). Yet if all we did was look at the present, with no regard for our future, there will certainly be no present in our future.

How do we prepare, if the forces of the universe are not impressed

by brick walls and guns?

By investing in

Truth

As far as I can tell, it beats the alternative.

Perhaps that is because I have absolutely no idea of what the alternative is.

The fountain of youth is self-awareness.
Its waters are imagination, fascination, and moderation.

R
I
G
H
T

Rule # 1: the one person you should never try to fool is yourself.

Rule # 2: if you never try fooling yourself, you'll never try fooling
anyone else.

Rule # 3: whether or not anyone else knows it, if you've been trying to
fool yourself you will be unfulfilled and unhappy.

Rule # 4: rule # 3 can be avoided by strict adherence to rule # 1.

How can we strictly adhere to rule #1?

Six feet above, by law. Unless you wish to be sprinkled around or kept on a mantle. Either way though, you - in this form - are gone. Hopefully you will have made the most of your experience.

Question: what is it that we each have the power to avoid, yet if we don't use our powers correctly can ruin our past, present, and future?

juggle

To decipher the word hidden in "juggle" follow these directions:

Add 8 letters to j. Subtract 16 letters from u. Add 11 letters to the

Second g. Subtract 7 letters from l. Add 15 letters to e.

T
I
M
E

Change is constant, but it is not

arbitrary; which means that it cannot

be the only constant in the universe.

Change follows

Truth;

Truth

follows

nothing

but itself. Strangely enough, in this respect it is unlike our perspective:

It is the product and cause of its self.

 Follow what is beyond theory and change.

Each passing moment will be right and nothing will be wasted.

When we allow ourselves to be embraced by solitude, seeds are germinated. We expect flowers to bloom immediately, but they don't. So we abandon the seeds whose growth require simply our attention. And we seek our experience only through the flowers others have grown.

Write down in order, the five most important things in the world to you.

1.

2.

3.

4.

5.

If you had three wishes (you can't wish for more) what would they be?

1.

2.

3.

What are five things you know to be absolutely, unquestionable truth?

1.

2.

3.

4.

5.

Write down your definition of the following words: Good. Bad. Need. Know.

1.

2.

3.

4.

Write down and explain who and what you are:

While traveling out of town one early evening, the master came across a former student busy selling wares from a storefront. "Hello master!" said the young man, proud to see his former teacher. "Good evening," said the master, "it appears as though you have quite a thriving business here." "Yes," replied the young man, "it is all mine and I am very busy making a lot of money." "Excellent!" said the teacher, "and do you still take the time to search within and cultivate the light?"

"No master," replied the student, "there is no longer any time for me to engage in such activity. If I am to get ahead I must focus all my energies on this business." "I see what you mean." said the master, smiling. "Well," he continued, "I must be on my way. It was very nice to see you. I wish you well in all your endeavors." The former student thanked the master and offered him his best wishes as well. Then, just as he was turning to go, the master pointed to the sky and said to his former student: "Notice the sun is setting. Will the light you seek lead you home through the dark?"

www.ingramcontent.com/pod-product-compliance
Lightning Source LLC
Chambersburg PA
CBHW031825090426
42741CB00005B/139

* 9 7 8 0 9 8 5 3 4 4 9 3 1 *